R.A. Whitehead

GLOSSOPS

Kings of Tarspraying

A History of W. & J. Glossop Ltd.

R.A. Whitehead & Partners

Tonbridge, Kent

2000

Fig.1. *The founder himself. William Glossop (1870-1930) in his Territorial Army uniform in a portrait that used to hang in the boardroom at Amisfield House.*

Published by R.A.Whitehead & Partners
42 Hadlow Road
Tonbridge, Kent TN9 1NZ

Photographs: Where not otherwise acknowledged the illustrations used came from the collections of Leon Birkett, the firm or of the author. Illustrations from other sources are acknowledged individually.

Cover: The cover illustration shows Atkinson sprayer No.102 (Works No.388 of 1923) and is taken from a drawing made by Mr. Dennis Boultwood of Communications Design Partnership by whom it was used in a Glossop advertising brochure. The drawing, it may be added, was not computer generated.

Typeset in Times New Roman 10 by J.E.Whitehead.

Printed and bound by Biddles Ltd., Woodbridge Park, Guildford, GU1 1DA

ISBN 0-9508298-X-5

Contents

Fig.2. *The machine that set the seal upon the success of the Glossop enterprise, Atkinson No.306, fleet No.101, the first wagon mounted sprayer to be delivered, with its driver, Frank Birkett (third from left) and the sweeping and gritting gang.*

Fig.3. *Here it is shown at a public demonstration for the benefit of visiting notables and the trade press on October 9, 1922, in Nunnery Lane, York. The three partners present, Arthur Rideal, William Glossop, and Henry Stephenson were on the left of the picture. As before the driver was Frank Birkett and the two men on the control platform were Walter Jones (left), foreman of the tar distillery, and Jim Fouracre.*

Leon Birkett (left) standing with Gordon Briggs, the company secretary and director at the Hipperholme head office, in the Works yard at Hipperholme in front of sprayer No.106, newly overhauled and repainted - the last steam driven sprayer to remain in Glossops' hands.

Foreword

by Leon Birkett, Esq. - former Depot Manager & Plant Supervisor at Hipperholme

Having spent forty years (1945-1985) working for W. & J. Glossop I must pay tribute to the author for his dedicated research into the workings of the firm from the boardroom down to the so-called sharp end where I spent my early days. It has brought back memories of events and places which were fading away in my mind and of men who have nearly all passed on. In my early days working with the road gangs life was rough and ready as were some of the men. Some were on the run from the wife or the law. Nevertheless there was generally a sort of esprit de corps. It was a gypsy sort of life but never humdrum.

Although I am not a dyed in the wool steam enthusiast (few of my contemporaries were) I can recommend this book for the wealth of detail in it concerning steam vehicles of various types and the part they played in the upkeep of roads in the early days.

Leon Birkett
Norwood Green, Yorkshire   February, 2000

Preface

What most of us refer to as 'tarring roads' the trade prefers to call 'surface dressing'. However described it is not a trade that has much attracted the attention of either historians or industrial archaeologists, most of such notice as it has received having come from historians of steam road vehicles with which, in the first half of the century, it was plentifully provided.

The firm of W. & J. Glossop Ltd. held a leading position in the surface dressing trade for some seventy-five years, having entered it more or less by accident when the joint founders, the brothers William and James Glossop, who had meant to set up in business as stone merchants and contractors for water-bound roads, encountered heavy obstacles in their intended path and turned instead to surface dressing. To refer to Glossops as 'kings of tarspraying' - a phrase they coined themselves - though not especially modest was reasonably accurate. There were several other good firms but few as big and certainly not many with such experience.

In the late nineteen seventies, by reason of friendship with one of the then directors who feared that in a period of turbulent change the firm's history might be lost, I was invited to write an account of its activities up to that time. This was done but when it was complete the intended publisher, Prince Marshall of Marshall, Harris & Baldwin, died. Soon afterwards Glossops became involved in the negotiations which led to the company being merged into the Colas group and, in consequence, the manuscript remained unpublished until 1999 when I again met Leon Birkett, the erstwhile plant superintendent of Glossops whom I had come to know during my earlier researches. Meeting Leon once more after a lapse of nearly twenty years so rekindled my enthusiasm for the project that I set about revising and recasting it with the result that is now before readers. Retirement and, in many cases, death have removed many of the Glossop people whom my wife and I met during the time of our research and for whom we had developed considerable respect and regard. This book is therefore a tribute to them.

Glossops bore the unmistakable imprints of their history. A high degree of individualism, a valuing of personal responsibility, great directness and absence of bureaucracy in the lines of communication were the distinguishing marks of the company from first to last. In an age accustomed to seeing executives spending only a year or two at a time in one organisation as they climbed the career structure it was reassuring to become closely acquainted with a company in which there was still great store set, both by the firm and by its staff, on continuity. In the course of business over some fifty years it fell to my lot to encounter numerous firms in which, ten years after first contact, not only was the man I had first dealt with no longer there but was not even recalled by the then generation of staff. Surface dressing, however, is one of those trades, like boilermaking, that is learned properly only by being with those who know it and knowledge of it is acquired, so to speak, as much through the pores of the mind by soaking up atmosphere as by conscious study. To be absorbed in ones job is one of the first steps towards contentment. Television and mass communication have killed what G.E. Evans called 'the oral tradition'. When men congregate, as they do less and less, in pubs they rarely share a common trade and shop is not much talked. In consequence we have largely thrown away our folk memory. In these pages I have tried to rescue a fragment.

Tonbridge, Kent
November, 1999

Robert A. Whitehead

Acknowledgements and Thanks

It is not until one comes to listing the people who have helped in writing this history that one realises how many have been involved. Firstly, of course, Digby Burnell, the Chairman, and his fellow directors were vital to the matter but it was Gordon Briggs, the company secretary as well as a director, who bore the brunt of my enquiries. Ernest Milner, his predecessor, was also a great help before his death in early 1978. Victor Jones, who had preceded Digby Burnell as chairman, gave valuable aid as, too, did Harry Peebles and E.R. Brewster, the retired directors at York and Bridgend respectively. Geoffrey Willsdon and Jean Rhys-Hughes (son and daughter of Frank Willsdon) were very helpful. William Glossop's nieces, Mrs. Nicholson and Mrs. Sykes, were very kind in sketching in family background, and William Brooke of Lightcliffe, son of Newton Brooke, William Glossop's employer before he set up on his own account, was similarly helpful. The company secretary's office of Shell UK Ltd. particularly Mrs. June Merrett, provided information on the absorption of W. & J. Glossop into the Shell Group as also did Mr. J. Wyatt, company secretary of Colas Ltd. Alan Duke of the Road Locomotive Society gave valuable help with information on the steam engines owned by the company and William Love, librarian of the Society, has also helped whilst the archivist of the Halifax Courier group provided from the paper's records the account of the death of James Glossop. Roger West, editor of *Steaming*, and Derek Rayner of the Road Roller Association also provided valued support. The staff of the West Yorkshire Archive Service were most helpful. Mr. Andrew Bunce, of Bunce (Ashbury) Ltd. went to great pains to provide, from his company's records, details of gritters supplied to Glossops. Leon Birkett, the depot manager and plant supervisor at Hipperholme, and Bob Walker, of the head office at Hipperholme, were able to provide much information from direct personal knowledge. Leon occupies a special place as during the revision of the manuscript I have had many discussions with him. I am also very grateful to him for contributing the foreword. Another factor which helped to clinch the matter of picking up the manuscript again was the encouragement given by my son-in-law, Michael Walters, who, as a young man, was a contract manager for Glossops. As he has done with many other of my books he has read and commented upon the manuscript and helped with the updating. Barry Macintosh Williams, whose father helped to coax William Glossop into selling his tar distillery to Yorkshire Tar Distillers, provided background information on the trade, as also did J.B.F. Earle. A lunch with the latter, during the time when he was writing his notable book *Black Top*, provided a fascinating back-stage picture of the road surfacing industry. To all who helped in any way, whether mentioned or not, I extend my heartiest thanks.

As ever my wife Jean was my companion and abettor in exploring the company archives, acting as type-setter and editor, and being my partner in our joint publishing enterprise. Without her enthusiastic support and collaboration I doubt if the work would have been completed.

Sources: The greater part of the information contained in this account is based upon the notes we made between 1977 and 1979 from the company's records at Amisfield House. When Amisfield House ceased to be the head office some sections of this mass of information were handed over to the West Yorkshire Archive Service, but I regret to say that a large proportion was destroyed. Nevertheless the sources, whether still extant or not are given in footnotes as they were at the time of our original researches.

Fig.4. James Glossop (1876-1908) began his working life on the Lancashire & Yorkshire Railway. This group showing the office staff of the goods department at Mirfield Station is thought to show the youthful James (front row right) with his older colleagues.

Fig.5. A view over the quarry at Horton-in-Ribblesdale.

Fig.6. Headlands Road, Liversedge, in August, 1907, after the completion of a stretch of Tarviated roadway using Glossops' Lembton granite and Tarvia mixed to Bristowe's specification. Surveyors were invited from all over the area. Some came in person but others sent their road foremen. Mr. F. Langley, the Liversedge surveyor, is the man on the extreme left. His foreman is the man in the cloth cap by the rear roll of the roller. James Glossop is on the forecarriage head of the roller and his brother William is leaning against the roll between James's feet.

Chapter 1

The Glossop Brothers

William Glossop was born in 1870, the son of James and Ellen Glossop of Mansfield. His father had been an engineer to a lead mine at Calver, Derbyshire, where he met his future wife, the daughter of Mr. Robert Cocker, landlord of the Derwentwater Arms, Calver, but before William's birth the lead mine had closed and James Glossop had joined the Nottinghamshire County Constabulary. William was born at Mansfield but subsequently the family moved to Mirfield, Yorkshire. William had four sisters, Alice, Anne, Susannah, and Nellie, and one brother, James, born at Mirfield in 1876[1].

Each of the brothers won a scholarship from elementary school to the Richard Thorpe Grammar School at Mirfield. Their early careers on leaving school are not recorded in detail. James is said to have worked for a while as a railway clerk in Mirfield but, from the first, William appears to have been attracted into stone quarrying. Certainly by the 1890s he was in the service of Brookes Ltd, at that time a very prominent stone quarrying firm in the North of England. Before long his brother, James, had also joined the same company.

Rooted in the York stone industry of the West Riding, Brookes Ltd had expanded into quarrying granite in Westmoreland, Guernsey, Norway and Sweden, supplying both road stone and masonry. The presiding members of the Brooke family were the brothers, Newton and Aspinall. Though there is little doubt that, like many comparable Victorian and Edwardian businesses, Brookes Ltd. was an autocratic empire, albeit with two emperors, the brothers did delegate departmental control to responsible managers in a considerable degree, reserving to themselves major policy decisions.[2] It would appear that the Brooke brothers were considerable judges of capability so that young men in their service were able to earn rapid promotion. William Glossop, being both sagacious and ambitious, climbed quickly not only in the scope of his duties but also in the degree of confidence reposed in him by his employers. On December 22, 1900, i.e. by the age of thirty, he was appointed secretary of the company with the status and authority virtually equivalent to that of a junior director, undertaking, besides the standard duties of company secretary, confidential missions on behalf of the board and having considerable business and social contacts with the surveyors and committee members of the Local Authorities - particularly in industrial Yorkshire and Lancashire - on whom the company depended for a high proportion of its trade.

About 1902 William met and subsequently married Emily Brewer, a woman some years his senior. William was somewhat maturer in his ways than his actual years and the fact that Emily was older than him does not seem to have interfered with their contentment. They set up home at Highfield, a substantial detached house on the ridge above Hipperholme, which William bought at auction on October 17, 1902, from Eli Titterington of Luddendenfoot. Without being palatial, the property was substantial[3] or, at least, comfortably roomy, and included a large hall, dining room, drawing room, kitchen, scullery, butler's pantry, four main bedrooms each with dressing room, attics, bathroom and W.C., good cellars, a three stall stable, loose box, coach house, harness room, and a four roomed cottage. Part of the purchase price was paid in cash and the vendor agreed to allow the remainder to remain on mortgage. In addition to this house William owned 5200 shares in Brookes Ltd. so that it may fairly be deduced that by the time of his marriage notwithstanding that he was only thirty-two years old, he was already a man of some personal substance and an important figure in the Brooke organisation.

In June, 1902, James Glossop married Theresa Morte of Barnsley, and it is perhaps a mark of his standing with Newton Brooke that the latter's wedding present to the young couple was a very fine set of solid silver dessert knives and forks with handles of mother-of-pearl, afterwards owned by his daughter, Mrs. Nicholson.[4]

With hindsight it is not difficult to perceive that William's lifetime ambitions could not have been contained within a career as a salaried official, no matter how trusted, in Brookes Ltd. It is also likely that even by the age of thirty-five executive responsibility had begun to develop the abrasive and autocratic side of his nature which was marked in his latter years and which, doubtless, made him progressively less qualified to serve Newton and Aspinall Brooke, themselves by no means lacking in similar attributes.

Without the parties realising it, therefore, their paths had begun to diverge. On the one hand the Brooke brothers continued to look upon William Glossop as a firmly placed and dependable foundation stone of their management structure whilst William, for his part, had begun to formulate the plans for the advancement of his career to being master of his own business.

Meanwhile his younger brother, James, had made a place for himself on the sales staff of Brookes Ltd. James was an easy going, free-spending man, of convivial habits though lacking, perhaps, the close grained tenacity of his brother but, by way of compensation, possessing the ability to be liked by all with whom he came into contact, valuable to him as a salesman. William seems to have conceded James's aptitude in selling even if, privately, he thought the easy charm of his brother was a cloak for an absence of self-discipline, and his final plan for setting up his own business included James as a partner, a decision that may have caused him some pangs in the next two or three years.

From such evidence as survives, principally the letters from William Glossop to Newton Brooke and to Schibsted, Brookes' manager in Scandinavia, cited more fully in chapter 2, it appears that the Glossop brothers had hoped to establish themselves as road contractors and stone merchants in a friendly but informal alliance with their former employers whereby the Glossops might have purchased their road materials from Brookes and sold stone, produced by the latter, on a purely merchanting basis. To William's horror his attempt to discuss his plans with Newton Brooke turned into a disastrous fiasco. To Newton Brooke it seemed that Glossop purposed to make use of the knowledge he had of the Brooke business and its customers to its detriment by the establishment of a directly and subversively competitive business. He was outraged that a man who for years had enjoyed his confidence and, in some degree, his friendship should seemingly so grossly abuse both. What William Glossop saw merely as a logical step in his personal progression the Brookes saw as a negligent or even dishonest use of the powers his position in Brookes Ltd. had given him. Therefore, instead of there being an orderly handing over of duties, William found his services summarily dispensed with, ostensibly for negligence, as from December 29, 1905.[5] James was not under the same cloud and resigned voluntarily at the end of January, 1906.

The stink of treachery was so powerful that the sweet smell of reason was overpowered. Had William ever had the opportunity of rational discussion with his erstwhile employer and of restoring a state of mutual respect the events narrated in Chapter 2 might have turned out very differently. The Glossops would very likely have laid the greater emphasis of their business strategy upon road surfacing and surface dressing contracts and not have embarked upon the quarrying enterprises which absorbed so much effort and capital and which brought them into competition with Brookes Ltd. As it was, however, the Glossops began their new venture overshadowed by the avowed hostility of their former employers and from the beginning were forced into the acquisition of their own quarries which, in the first ten years of their undertaking, were to prove the source of great hindrances to their peace of mind.

Socially the brothers seem to have been conformists. William led the kind of life and maintained the sort of establishment expected of a man in his position and of his day. Recreationally, however, he was austere. As young men both brothers had been keen Rugby League players and William continued to support the game after he had ceased to play, but once he dropped playing Rugby a round of golf or an occasional game of bowls was his only sport. The Glossops cultivated the acquaintance of those from whom they might have been expected to gain commercial advantage - local authority engineers and surveyors and chairmen and members of committees - with some of whom, no doubt, there was unfeigned friendship. This meant much travelling and a good deal of wining and dining, mostly by Jimmy though enough was undertaken by William to cause Emily Glossop to complain, as is evident from asides in various letters in William's letter book, that he was away so much that she might well have been his widow.

Both men were Freemasons, and members of the Elland Division, Saville Lodge. The parchment certificate[6] admitting James to membership is dated 1906. William took a prominent part in Masonic matters - it was difficult for him to be a follower in anything - and was an office holder in his Lodge. After the death of James, as narrated in Chapter 2, he was gravely disappointed by the treatment of his brother's widow by the Lodge. Like many young and ambitious men newly embarked upon what seemed likely to be a lucrative career James had not calculated upon dying young and in consequence had made but slender provision for Theresa whom, William considered, might legitimately have looked to her late husband's Lodge for funds to help her over her worst difficulties - funds which in the event were not forthcoming. In consequence of his dissatisfaction William resigned from the Lodge.

Jimmy - as he was invariably known both to relatives and business acquaintances - was the salesman of the pair, William the austere and anxious administrator. How they fared in their partnership is the subject of the next chapter. Though they travelled and spent freely when on business the brothers seem to have considered holidays an indulgence and, as far as can be ascertained, neither took real holidays nor travelled abroad. One weeks holiday a year, taken out of the spraying season, was the Glossop rule for staff even until after the 1939-45 war, but the partners treated themselves no differently in this respect.

[1] Personal letter from Mrs. D. Sykes, niece of William Glossop, to the author 21.11.77

[2] Personal letter to the author from Mr. W.A.N. Brooke (son of Newton Brooke) 28.7.77

[3] Particulars issued by the auctioneers, Walter Holdsworth & Son, filed at Amisfield House.

[4] Personal communication from Mrs. Nicholson (née Glossop) to the author 2.1.78

[5] Letter from Mr. W.A.N. Brooke to author 14.7.77

[6] Certificate in possession of Mrs. M. Nicholson.

Fig. 7. William Glossop's great interest was the working of the Elland Edge flag rock.
This is the firm's Landemere quarry at Northowram.

Fig.8. The Whalley mixing pan in which the Glossop brothers produced the 'fine tar topping' for the binding course in a Tarviated road, a system which formed the foundation of the good name they came to enjoy for their road-making.

Fig.9. Jimmy Glossop, seen here in the conservatory of his house in Cobden Terrace, Hipperholme, had the great talent of being liked by nearly everyone he met, an invaluable attribute in a salesman though his free-spending habits were his brother's despair.

Chapter 2

The New Enterprise

As a realist William Glossop could not have expected the Brooke brothers to have been pleased at his decision to set up his own business. It is doubtful, however, if he had anticipated the furore under which his departure had actually taken place nor the brothers' total repudiation of him. As he later commented in a letter to a former colleague:[1]

> A more business-like way of looking at my separation would have been to have recognised it and worked together. It would have been the best for both sides but they would not.

The outraged feelings of the Brookes can scarcely have been assuaged by his setting up his new business in Hipperholme. Since he lived there and had many business friends and acquaintances in the town and district it was natural enough on his part not to move but in retrospect it is possible to see how being cooped up with him in the same town of some 4250 inhabitants must have irked his former employers.

Because the Brooke brothers' system of management had allowed the responsible departmental managers wide discretion in day to day decisions, reserving only wider matters of policy to themselves, what they came increasingly to regard as William Glossop's duplicity faced them with the onerous decision of whether or not this system had to be changed. To have continued it meant that the risk remained of history repeating itself, whilst to have amended it would have necessitated taking into their own hands a large volume of routine management matters for which they had neither taste nor aptitude. Initial anger over, William Glossop's breach of confidence, as they saw it, and exasperation at his subsequent actions led them to look questioningly at how he had conducted himself whilst in their employment. As has been noted, trading with public authorities in the opening years of this century was a very personal affair, particularly in the smaller Urban and Rural District Councils where there might be no other staff concerned in road work than the Surveyor. The representatives of firms doing business, or aspiring to do business, with a council had to be at pains to be known to the surveyor and committee members whose goodwill had to be courted by assiduous attention, which meant regular visits and, usually, regular entertainment, if no other favours. Whilst at Brookes Ltd. William had had to bear his share of this expenditure for which he had claimed, and received, reimbursement from his employers. He now found himself faced with a challenge from Newton and Aspinall Brooke to give account of how certain of these monies had been spent. This matter remained in dispute throughout 1906. In mid-October the Brookes' solicitors gave notice that unless the sums in dispute were re-paid their principals would sell the shares that Glossop held in Brookes Ltd. 'as they thought fit' to satisfy the account. This led him to fear that the shares, representing a major portion of his capital, would be slaughtered for a fraction of their true value, a threat countered, on solicitor's advice, by a writ. [2]

Whether or not his erstwhile employers would have carried their campaign to those lengths is a matter which cannot now be known. Certainly William Glossop perceived it as a real threat. On the advice of his solicitors, Clarkson & Buckley of Halifax, he took the step of paying £557.9.2, representing the disputed sum, into court.[3] How the dispute was settled is uncertain. Though references to it continued to appear in correspondence in 1907 and 1908 no evidence can be found in the County Court records at Halifax of its having been brought to trial. When I discussed it with Walter Brooke, son of Newton Brooke, he was of the opinion[4] that, once the feelings of his father and uncle had had a couple of years to cool, it was settled between the parties out of court, most likely by its being dropped by the Brooke brothers. Probably it was better for both sides that it was, for a trial of the action would have resulted in the washing of much soiled linen in public to the embarrassment of both sides. Whilst there were not likely to have been many undisguised bribes there would inevitably have been much disclosure of how far Brookes Ltd. had been prepared to go to win favour with its customers. From William's point of view also, no matter how the points in dispute were decided in court, there was almost bound to have been a tarnishing of his character.

A second action, alleging breach of his contract of service with Brookes Ltd. by setting up in Hipperholme as a stone merchant in opposition to them, dragged on for some time without coming to a hearing and Walter Brooke believed that this, too, was settled out of court. In addition to the threat of these two actions William Glossop was subjected to a further hindrance in that, at the annual general meeting in May, 1906, Brookes Ltd. passed the dividend for 1905, though up to that time the dividend record of the company had varied between 5% and 7%. Glossop concluded that this action was aimed at causing him financial embarrassment as in his opinion[5] the earnings in 1905 had been sufficient to justify a dividend of more than 20%.

Not only were these matters a burden of worry to William Glossop but also the means of pinning down a considerable part of his capital, necessitating borrowing on a considerable scale to finance his new operations. In part this came from the Commercial Bank, Halifax,[6] but in part from friends and relatives. Notwithstanding these unexpected obstacles William and James Glossop began trading on February 1, 1906, as stone merchants and road contractors. They also set up a subsidiary firm, the Penyghent Stone Co., with works in a quarry at Penyghent near Horton in Ribblesdale where, inter alia, they made artificial stone paving flags with a non-slip surface, sold under the brand name of *Economic*. In this they were in outright competition with Brookes Ltd. who had a large trade in their own non-slip flags and a very high reputation for the quality of their product. The Penyghent quarry was leased from Lord Leconfield and was taken over from James Delaney of Settle, with whom an arrangement was entered into for a period of joint trading with progressive acquisition of the capital by Glossops. Because of the pressures on their liquidity, arising in part from the legal entanglements with Brookes Ltd. but also from the fact that trading for the year 1906-07 produced a nett loss, these capital repayments were to become a millstone.

Also, since the possibility no longer existed of a trading arrangement with Brookes Ltd. in respect of granite road metal they had to cast around for an alternative source of supply. Early in 1907, in partnership with Martin L. Boundy of Bassenthwaite, they secured an interest in the Close Quarry at Embleton, Cumberland, for the products of which they coined the brand name *Lembton* a near anagram of the place name. It would seem that it was into this enterprise, known and incorporated subsequently as the Cumberland Granite Co. Ltd., that William put the monies borrowed on second mortgage of his house, Highfield, Hipperholme.

To add to his troubles at the end of December, 1906, William partially dislocated his knee which hampered physical movement, and whilst convalescing he wrote to Newton Brooke on January 17, 1907, in a last attempt to bring reason back into their relationship:

Dear Mr. Brooke,

It is strange that notwithstanding your promise and my several reminders to meet me in Leeds I haven't had a line from you. If it were not that I am lame and have been for some weeks through an accident I should have come over to Arkley but at present I am having to spare myself as much as possible.

For the life of me I cannot understand the cause of such treatment, or the slightest reason for it. If we cannot do business together surely we know one another well enough to be friends and I have done nothing to forfeit your friendship which I value more than the mere chance of buying business.

As I told you before I want a talk with you and I should be glad if you meet me in Leeds. I will try to make your time suitable.

I feel very sore that you have served me so badly without any cause or reason that I know of at all. If there is anything then tell me frankly and let us see if it can't be put straight.

Yours sincerely
Will Glossop

Nor was he helped by his brother's free and easy attitude to money. Within the partnership William undertook responsibility for administration and James for sales, but the contrasting temperaments of the two men made it difficult for them to work harmoniously. The dominant William, the Territorial Army officer and terror of office boys, the estimator who would work to the third decimal place of an old penny, and the thrifty gatherer-in of credits on empty barrels and packing cases, found his brother's carefree attitude to money irresponsible as, indeed, it often was. On April 30, 1907, he remonstrated with James on his level of expenditure:

Dear James,

Notwithstanding previous incidents I see you have again drawn cheques for £21.10.0 for your own purposes without a word of consent or otherwise from me.

It betokens little or no regard for the business, as it means some accounts which ought to have been paid having to stand over, another step in the wrong direction.

Last month I see you had a few pounds over £50 and I have had to manage on twenty. I think £25 per month should cover everything you need and have to pay and I will try to make £30 serve my purposes, and I shall certainly not agree to your having any more.

It is a confounded shame that a brother should have to need such a step as this to be taken knowing the circumstances as you do. Go through your sales for the past six months and see if you have earned what you have drawn.

The cheque you have drawn to pay nine months rent of your own house is some evidence of mismanagement of your own private affairs. You have had ample monies to pay your own liabilities in due course during the last 15 or 16 months and you have had something like £600/£700. You know best whether such a sum has been required and profitably spent.

Yours, Wm. Glossop

When James needed more cash he simply wrote and signed a cheque on the partnership account, whether or not the money was due to him or could be afforded. William wrote again, icily, on October 31, 1907:

J.G.

I see you have drawn two more cheques without my knowledge. Once more and finally I tell you that it is not agreeable to me and I hope you will on no account do it again.

I see you have had over £40 in cash besides two cheques this month. How you have spent it perhaps you know but I don't and I don't agree to your drawings being more than the amount mentioned some time ago, £25, unless very special circumstances.

We cannot afford such expenses and you must not lose sight of the fact that such withdrawals are leaving you debtor to the business instead of acquiring a share of it.

Yours,
Will

James undoubtedly secured orders but, unfortunately, at the expense of cutting rates and agreeing discounts such that William could not make the work pay when secured - the perennial disagreement between sales and production. He had already commented, with the chilliness which increasingly marked his notes to his brother, on April 30, 1907:

If you can't get orders on a profitable basis it is surely better to leave them alone and I neither want nor will have them.

James probably considered, of course, that William underestimated the problems which had to be faced in selling the services of a new firm, which had yet to lay down a reputation, in competition with established companies of known repute. William, moreover, must have known from his own experience and, indeed, from the subject of his current dispute with Newton Brooke that the distribution of largesse was a very nearly inevitable pre-requisite of sales. In writing *Black Top* J.B. Earle unearthed the following treasure from a local newspaper of December, 1902 which illustrates the point:

It being proposed to obtain Quenast (Belgian) granite, Mr. G. said it was a beastly shame, for the sake of 2d. to go in for foreign granite prepared by foreign labour.

Mr. B. suggested that the qualities of the granite should be tested by sections being put down lengthways with the different granites.

Mr. W : I think the best test is to inquire which Company gives the best dinners (Laughter).

Mr. D : There is something in that.

Mr. M : We thought Forest Rock gave a good dinner last year.

Mr. P : This foreign company does not give dinners.

That he did recognise these problems is clear from a paragraph in a letter he wrote on December 6, 1906, to John Kerr, manager of the Halifax Commercial Bank (the firm's bankers):

A lot of our time this year is being spent sowing the seed for next year and, although as in every other trade merit must count, without the goodwill of those in authority merit alone would have small chance, so the opening of a new business in our line is always extraordinarily expensive.

James undoubtedly enjoyed his wining and dining and the social contacts he made. He was in charge of the firm's stand at the Building Trades Exhibition at Olympia (London) when it was visited by the Prince and Princess of Wales (the future King George V and Queen Mary) on April 6, 1907. Told by James that the *Economic* stone on show had a non-slip finish the literal and practical Prince insisted that the flags be arranged in a disorderly heap at steep angles so that he could climb over it to test this alleged property. Nevertheless there was undeniable substance in William's claim that money was being spent on a scale that exceeded what was necessary or productive. The trading figures for the first year showed, before attributing any payment to the proprietors for management salaries, a nett loss of £828 on a turnover of £2351. What were euphemistically called 'Travelling expenses' amounted to £811. The proprietors divided the loss equally between them and endeavoured to do better the next year.

One must conclude that Jimmy paid only lip service to reform. On September 2, 1907, William had reached the point at which he drafted - but, in the end, did not send - a letter to James in the following terms, terminating the partnership:

Dear Sir,

I hereby give you notice that on and from this date the partnership between us is dissolved.

Accounts shall be taken by Mr. Kerr and if any monies are found to be due to you I am agreeable to pay or to accept payments from you, the payment in each case to be made at once.

The purchaser shall have the exclusive right to the use of the titles under which the business has hitherto been carried on except that of W. & J. Glossop and in that case the purchaser shall not have the right to the other name.

No value shall be taken of good will.

Yours truly

William Glossop

After a reprimand James seems to have charmed his brother round and the uneasy partnership continued.

The firm's trading was given a useful fillip by a well-chosen technical decision made by the Glossop brothers in 1907. Away from larger town centres, where pavings of tarmacadam, stone setts, wood blocks or asphalt were commonly in use, in the opening years of the twentieth century road wearing courses were generally of water bound macadam - this is to say a broken stone bed held together by intimate physical contact between the pieces and by the presence of a binding material such as fine aggregate, sand, hoggin, chalk or plain earth in the interstices. The best of the native and imported roadstones, referred to, with a fine disregard for geological accuracy, as the granites, which broke to a cubiform shape with rough surfaces, bound together well under a heavy roller with minimal additions of binders but because granite wearing courses were expensive in the first cost (though lower on maintenance) less desirable types of stone, being cheaper and, often, locally produced, were frequently preferred, particularly for secondary roads. The use of local stone in preference to granites was a subject touching on local politics, especially where the owners of quarries were local rate-payers or influential people or where the quarries were a substantial source of employment. Consequently it could be the subject of persuasion, lobbying, and, it is feared, quite often downright bribery.

The importance of this to the present narrative is that the less suitable a stone was for water bound macadam roadwork the greater was its potential for creating dust as softer stones broke down more readily into dust under the actions of frost and traffic whilst their reduced self-binding capacity heightened the need for added binder with its concomitant generation of dust. With the arrival of substantial numbers of rubber tyred motor cars - eight and a half thousand private cars by March, 1904 - those responsible for road maintenance soon found that whilst a steel tyre, if not loaded to excess, consolidated a water bound carriageway, by contrast the driven rubber type, because of its pliable characteristics, tended in part to envelop the particles and loosen them from the surface of the roadway, thereby adding to the dust. At the same time, in dry weather the air turbulence created by the speed of the vehicle raised the dust in clouds. Summer dust had long been a nuisance. All kinds of palliatives had been tried varying from simple watering with a water cart to sprinkling with aqueous solutions of various chemicals and, finally, to coating with oils and tars. Of these, by far the most effective and long lasting was to brush away the dust, coat the surface with hot coal tar and blind it with sand or fine grit.

At first crude tar, mostly from local gas works but some provided by coke ovens, was used but lack of uniformity in its composition made it an unpredictable material in performance, whilst the phenols present in it were carried away in rainwater washings off the road which polluted watercourses to the detriment of fish life and, indeed, of animals or human beings drinking the water. Crude tar coatings had a short life, one winter being usually sufficient to break them up. If they contained an excess of carbon, this disintegration produced an objectionable black powder. Furthermore, the presence of water or ammoniacal liquors in the crude tar could lead to foaming in the tar boiler with consequential over flowing and ignition of the tar by the fire under the boiler.

For this reason dehydration of crude tar was a valuable first step but a more radical improvement was secured by distilling the crude tar and blending the resulting heavier fractions to produce a reasonably uniform product of predictable viscosity. Most of the early distilled tars were sold as proprietary articles. R.S. Clare & Co.Ltd. of Liverpool began marketing their *Tarco A* in 1904 and were soon followed by F.E. Bristowe who had his *Tarvia* made for him by a number of distillers. The performance of these proprietary tars remained relatively poor by comparison with the more sophisticated products of the nineteen-thirties but they offered to road engineers a very marked improvement over crude or merely dehydrated gas tar, not least in that they reduced, in a considerable degree, variations as between batch and batch. Further betterment waited upon detailed research and identification of the characteristics that required to be amended. The degree of quality control brought about by early proprietary tars was thus purely relative. Regulation of their properties was largely achieved by adjusting specific gravity since the importance of viscosity had not yet been fully appreciated and, in any event, the Hutchinson tar viscometer, which made accurate measurement of viscosity possible, did not appear until 1911. The preparation of *Tarvia*, the proprietary tar which was to become closely involved in the Glossop story, involved the cutting back of the heavier fractions of distilled tar by means of additives supplied to the distiller by Bristowe. The composition of the additives was his trade secret but they are likely to have consisted of a blend of the higher fractions of distillation.[7]

Trials of dust palliatives conducted at Staines under the auspices of the Road Improvement Association at Whitsun, 1907, poorly organised though they were, demonstrated that hot tar was the only practical material for the purpose of dust control. The prize for tars went to R.S. Clare & Co. but Bristowe's *Tarvia* created sufficient impression upon S.W. Manning, the Surveyor to Staines R.D.C. to cause him to make a more ambitious experiment, itself a continuation of a limited trial made by his friend and colleague Arthur Gladwell, Surveyor to the neighbouring Eton R.D.C. Each of the men had seen and recognised the merits of tarmacadam as a surfacing material, both straightforward coated stone and Purnell Hooley's patented *Tarmac* based on slag aggregate, but found the cost of either beyond the restricted road budgets of the respective councils. *Tarvia* was offered for use as either a straight surface dressing or as 'fine tar topping', a slack mixture of one-third binder with two-thirds fine granite chippings, which set by loss of volatiles and absorption of binders into the base when used as a topping for footpaths.

In the late summer of 1906 Gladwell had laid a small section of roadway in which he had used a compound of this latter description - but not, as far as one can tell, made of Bristowe's materials - to bind a layer of new broken stone to an old road surface. In the more extended experiment at Staines Manning and Gladwell first coated the old road with a generous layer of the binder mix on which they distributed a layer of 2¼" Quenast granite at the rate of one ton to ten and a half square yards, rolling it with a water ballasted roller until the binder began to show through the topping. They then filled the surface with binder and rolled it solid with a moistened horse-drawn roller. When the material had hardened they rolled it with a steam-roller. The area of the experiment was 4360 square yards. Work began on July 17 and was completed on August 7. The report which Manning made to his committee was printed at length in *The Surveyor* for August 30, 1907. In it he concluded that the *Tarviated* road had cost him 1s.9d (8.75p) per square yard compared with 1s.6½d (7.71p) for a water-bound granite topping, a result which, given the improved wearing surface of the road, justified his very evident self-satisfaction.

F.E. Bristowe, too, was pleased with the result and the resultant publicity which, no doubt, he cultivated assiduously. Gladwell and Manning seem to have enjoyed the notice their experiment received but not to have sought to capitalise upon it by a patent or otherwise. Gladwell, a native of Macclesfield, is reputed to have been a cheerful and likeable man more interested in promoting his system as a means of road improvement than in his personal aggrandisement, though as a result of the road at Staines and some others at Slough and Stoke Poges he achieved extended mention in *The Times* of March 24, 1908, and considerable attention in the trade press. On the crest of this wave of interest in *Tarviated* roads William and James Glossop secured from Bristowe a licence to lay his materials in the North of England. How the matter was arranged is not recorded nor is the extent of their territory, but the alliance marked the turning point in their fortunes, launching them into the new sphere of black top road-works and away from the desperately competitive field of stone quarrying and selling.

Before the autumn of 1907 set in a road had been resurfaced on Gladwell's system at nearby Liversedge and in May, 1908, a stretch was done in Hipperholme itself where, the previous autumn, the quality of material supplied under contract for its water-bound roads and general methods of road maintenance had been the subject of a particularly acrimonious discussion in the Council. This work at Hipperholme was followed by a stretch of road at Balby in July, 1908, undertaken mainly as an experiment for the West Riding County Council. James Glossop, always at his best in these matters, organised a considerable assembly of councillors and road surveyors from all over South Yorkshire whom he afterwards entertained, in a manner described as 'lavish', at the Plough Hotel, to which he enticed his elder brother who made a soberly worded but effective speech on the advantages of the Gladwell system. It was James, however, who led some of the guests to the bowling green [8] and the drinking party that followed.

By the time the stretch at Balby was laid William had telescoped somewhat the method of constructing the *Tarvia Sandwich*, eliminating Manning's water ballasted roller and horse roller by doing all the rolling with a steam-roller, doubtless adjusting his mixes to suit. In consequence his cost per square yard had come down from 2s.4d. (11.67p) at Liversedge in 1907 to 1s.6½d (7.71p) at Hipperholme.[9] In these contracts the brothers used Embleton granite from Close Quarry, drying the fine chippings used to make the matrix but not the 2¼" stone; the weakness from the cohesion point of view of Gladwell's system. Apart, however, from operating Gladwell's method of resurfacing using Tarvia as the binder the terms of the licence from Bristowe to the Glossops appear to have embraced the selling of his tar on a commission basis in their area and also the undertaking of surface dressing using Tarvia. What the limits of the area were is no longer clear. The surviving correspondence suggests that Lancashire and Yorkshire and, possibly, Cumberland were covered but gives no hint as to how much more of the North of England was included.

The end of the year 1907 saw a turn-round to profitable trading with resultant improvement in the relationship between William and James and a general easing of financial tension. During 1907 William had been forced to temporise with Delaney over the payment of the monies due to the latter from the operation of the Horton in Ribblesdale quarry. William admitted frankly that he did not have the means of paying over the capital sums as they became due though he was able and willing to pay interest on them. Faced with the prospect of rescinding the deal and taking back the quarry or alternatively accepting deferred payment plus interest Delaney, of course, desired neither. He was an elderly man and probably wanted only peace and quiet. Early in 1908 William suggested that they should meet to talk the matter over but Delaney declined and, in consequence, on February 21 Will Glossop wrote to him at Settle formally terminating the agreement between them over the quarry. He delivered this letter by hand, having apparently arranged with Delaney to meet him on the platform at Settle railway station where, because of the bad lighting and Delaney's failing sight, he had to read it to him. As William explained, his inability to pay the sum of £1000 which had become due to Delaney on February 1 arose from the refusal of Brookes Ltd. to declare a dividend for 1906, when he had reasonable grounds for expecting not less than a 5% dividend on his holding of 5200 shares. On his return to Hipperholme, in a letter dated February 22, he went on to say 'we believe that no dividends have been paid since we left the Company simply to harass and injure us as much as possible'. Delaney agreed, for the time being, to accept deferred payment and the storm blew over.

The state of the partnership relations seems to have improved or, at least, become quieter during 1908. The emergence of surface dressing as an important, although seasonal, element of the business reduced the dependence of the brothers upon the heavily competitive stone trade. Though the amount of eating and drinking done by road surveyors at the brothers' expense doubtless rankled as much with William as it had ever done he could no longer object that it was unproductive, and James continued on his convivial way until the morning of October 21.

That morning, in his usual health and spirits, notwithstanding the many problems they were still facing on the financial front, he left the office to go to Halifax and thence on to Leeds for various meetings. He caught the 11.05 a.m. train from Halifax on the Lancashire & Yorkshire Railway. At Lightcliffe he was noted asleep in a compartment but at Lowmoor, the next stop, the carriage door was found swinging open and the compartment empty. All traffic was stopped, the line was searched, and he was found on the track alive but frightfully mutilated. Taken to Bradford Infirmary he lived only until the afternoon. At the subsequent inquest a verdict of accidental death was returned[10] though, it appears, there was a sustained whispering campaign in the town suggesting that his death was suicide. William devoted considerable effort to dealing with one offender prominent in the life of the town.[11] Subsequently he entered a claim, on behalf of Jimmy's widow, against the Lancashire & Yorkshire Railway[12] alleging negligence by the staff in failing to secure the carriage door.

The death of James was a great shock to William. He wrote to Martin Boundy, their partner in the Embleton enterprise, 'It has made my aims and objects in life look very small and it has made me realise too how necessary it is for one to do whilst he is alive all he can for the protection and guidance of those left behind.' Predictably James had done nothing to provide for his widow, Theresa, and children beyond a small insurance policy and his share in the firm which amounted to £660.17s.4d.[13] nor did he own the house in Cobden Terrace where he lived. His wife had to move to a much smaller establishment and William undertook the upholding of the family. The two girls, Marjory and Dorothy, became effectively wards of William and Emily who had no children of their own. Early in 1910 William wrote to a fellow mason 'My brother's widow was left unprovided for with two small children' but by reason of his own generosity the girls were well educated and saw no want.

William and Boundy selected a substantial slab of their own Cumberland granite which was dressed and erected as a memorial to his brother in 1909. At the time that James died plans were well in hand for incorporating the Embleton quarry as a limited company and this was completed before the end of the year. The subscribers named in the incorporation of the Cumberland Granite Co. Ltd. registered on December 10, 1908, were Mr. & Mrs. William Glossop; Theresa Glossop (James's widow); Martin Boundy and his wife, Mary; James Hunter of Hipperholme; Arthur Wood of Bradford; and Charles Sheard of Prestwick.

The differences over the Horton quarry, which had been momentarily damped down, had continued to smoulder and were eventually taken to court by Delaney. In writing to Boundy on October 29, 1908, William told him the case had been referred to an Arbitrator and was, therefore, likely to take a long while. In fact, it was not until the following May that the matter was resolved. In the meantime he became involved in an action against the Midland Railway company over freight rates. Though this was eventually settled on terms favourable to William Glossop the drain on his finances was as heavy as that on his energy. Fortunately the tolerant Fred Bristowe tided him over by not pressing for payment of his accounts which he allowed to build up to over £1300 during the winter of 1908/09 when William was distributing Tarvia for use during the ensuing summer of 1909. Whilst comparisons of the value of money at different times are not simple and vary according to the elements taken into account in the calculations it is probably the case ninety years later that this figure of £1300 in 1908/09 would be equivalent to not less than £65000, a sizeable sum by the standard of the sizes of the respective businesses, and even when well established and prosperous William Glossop did not forget Bristowe's kindness to him when he was struggling.

The hearing of the case of Delaney v. Glossop did not go well from the latter's point of view. The foreman of the works, on whom he relied for evidence, turned out to be a poor witness and became rattled under cross-examination. As William wrote to Boundy, whom he made his confidant in this as in many other matters, in a letter dated May 27, 1909:

> This man had previously worked for Delaney for a number of years, lives in one of Delaney's houses and hopes to be taken on by Delaney. He was my only witness and I knew I ran a risk of his trying to run with both sides but I was bound to

take him to prove certain facts. After he had done this and the other side began to cross-examine him he began to prevaricate and eventually got so much mixed up that he hardly knew what he was saying. He was a rotten witness and I did not forget to tell him what I thought of his despicable ways.

Fortunately, on the off-chance of their being needed, William had taken along some of his foreman's letters to him which the latter, on re-examination, had to admit disproved what, under cross-examination, he had said to Glossop's detriment but, by destroying his credibility as a witness, this also made his evidence for Glossop valueless.

In the same letter in which these troubles were poured out to Boundy William arranged to meet him over the Whitsun holiday at Horton and walk down the railway to Settle to inspect outcrops of rock, similar to that at Horton, which Boundy, the expert quarryman, had observed from the train. William hurriedly borrowed a 4" scale Ordnance Survey of the route from a neighbour, Mr. Aldridge, and marked several promising locations pointed out by Boundy. As a result of the walk he wrote exploratory letters to three landowners in Ribblesdale on June 3. As William had predicted the court case over Horton went against him and he had to give up the works. This apart - and it was bad enough - he had to find a sum of the order of £650 for Delaney's costs, plus his own. On January 21, 1910, the Friday before the Monday in which the Taxing Master's certificate as to Delaney's costs was due to be signed, William wrote to a friend 'It now raises the question whether I should try to pay them or whether I should file my petition' - such was the state of low spirits to which he had been reduced. The depression was short lived, however, and the will to fight was revived by the offer of financial help.

On Boundy's advice he had leased new ground at Horton for the extraction of stone and had set up on it a modern crushing and screening plant. By February, 1910, he was, in the course of letters to Surveyors, inviting them to inspect the new and up-to-date equipment. Once again Bristowe helped him out by refraining from pressing for money. On June 8, 1909, his conscience pricked by his continuing reliance on Bristowe's patience, William had offered him as security five hundred fully paid one pound shares in the Cumberland Granite Co. Ltd. but there is no evidence that Bristowe took up the offer.

Tarvia was basking in the sunshine of extended approbation amongst road surveyors but as technical knowledge of the desirable composition and behaviour characteristics of road tars became more widely disseminated the regard which Bristowe's product enjoyed became more dependent upon appreciation of his personal commercial integrity than upon the actual composition of his product. On February 17, 1910, William Glossop met Mr. Kirby, the Borough Engineer of Batley[14] - a faithful adherent of Tarvia. In discussing the characteristics of tars Kirby remarked that if he so desired he could at any time make a compound tar similar to Tarvia but showed Glossop a specification he had prepared for his committees which meant effectively that, without Tarvia being mentioned by name, only it would satisfy the specification. William borrowed a copy of the specification and sent it anxiously to Bristowe to see if it was as watertight as Kirby imagined. Competition for surface dressing contracts in the North of England was becoming very keen and Tarvia needed friends. Glossops' two principal local competitors, Brothertons and Ellisons, pushed the price lower and lower. An inevitable concomitant of keen prices was extreme economy of application. Prices were so low that quality, particularly coverage per gallon, had to suffer. In the end, the effect on the Glossop business was that it expanded further and further afield, into less competitive areas but died off at the centre. Compositions such as *Tarvia* and Clare's *Tarco* were anyway being overhauled by improvements in general road tars from other makers, a change of emphasis that the institution of the Road Board in 1910 hastened. The Road Board was not a lively organisation but it performed a useful service to local authorities in issuing the first general specification for road tars, in which Tar No.1 was designed for surface dressing. After it appeared the proprietary brands of tar suffered a steady waning of importance in the face of standard tars.

In the summer of 1910 the Cumberland Granite Co. Ltd. had a winding-up order made against it, under which E.R.C. Kerr, the company's accountant, of Barum Top, Halifax, was appointed liquidator. Charles Sheard, a friend and fellow share holder in the British Water Main & Sewer Cleaning Co. Ltd., agreed to put up £150 for Glossop to bid, in the name of his wife, for the plant, stock-in-trade, and unexpired lease. In view of what followed this must have been a wholly inadequate offer but Kerr, nevertheless. seems to have accepted it. However, after agreeing to it he changed his mind on receiving a further and better offer from two friends of Boundy. The upshot was a court action by William Glossop to enforce the first sale, in which he lost the day, the judge deciding that the Liquidator had acted rightly in disregarding the alleged first sale. Consequently Glossop, who still wanted the quarry, had to pay a higher price plus costs, bringing him again to the verge of bankruptcy. Once more Fred Bristowe's forbearance staved off catastrophe. Writing to thank him on May 18, 1912, William said:

> I had plenty of offers to make a new start and if I had studied my own convenience, and no one else, I should have done so but I could never have met you or other friends again and I should have missed the guidance of the true friendship I have met with at the hands of yourself and one or two others which I value so much.

In buying the assets and setting up a new company William had secured as a partner P.W. Spencer, a lime merchant and quarry owner of Skipton. Spencer seems to have believed in the future possibilities of the quarry and in Glossop's managerial and entrepreneurial capacity but, on the other hand, he was wary of his notoriously litigious disposition and had no wish, moreover, to become enmeshed in the tangled skein of William's other financial and business affairs. Accordingly his agreement to contribute to the quarry was very carefully worded.

It was not until two days before Christmas, 1912, that William wrote to Charles Sheard, who had put up part of the money for him to continue in business:

> I have at last got the quarry affair practically cleared up. In buying it over I am something like £450 out of pocket, perhaps more. To buy it I had to pay about £350 all told and the Bank of course had to advance it. I anticipated that when I got some of it back that they would let me use the surplus, whatever it was, over the overdraft there was before they advanced the money but they have not done so and this has crippled me and prevented my clearing off the account as I intended. Then again you will remember Spencers did not agree to pay the £1250 purchase of half share in the quarry until they had completed the equipment of the quarry and then only if there was any balance left. They tell me that the whole and more has been expended. Of course it has made the quarry more valuable but it has tied my hands again. Nevertheless, with all these things, I think matters are coming round very nicely. ...

The end of 1912, however, really marked the watershed of his troubles as far as money was concerned for he did not need to borrow money again nor temporise with his creditors on the scale of the previous six years, although three years later he did face one further major threat which came about in this fashion. In the summer of 1911, when still pressed on all sides by problems, he had been approached by an employee of his competitors, Ellisons, who had their own tar distillery, to see if he also would consider setting up a distillery sufficient to produce the considerable volume of tar that he was, by then, using in his surface dressing contracts. Fierce bargainer though he was William felt honour compelled him to consult Bristowe, to whose tolerant attitude his survival owed so much.[15] The latter, it seems, raised no objection to the proposal and agreed to Tarvia being produced in the new works when set up. The upshot was an arrangement with the York Gas Company whereby William Glossop and four partners set up a distillery at York Gas Works. The four partners he took in this enterprise were Harold P. Hird of Hipperholme, Thomas Hammond, Clifford Richardson and Edgar Chambers, all of Huddersfield, who were themselves in partnership as Hird, Chambers & Hammond in Market Street, Huddersfield. Hird bought out the shares of Hammond, Richardson and Chambers, and was himself ultimately bought out by Glossop in March, 1918, continuing, however, in the surface dressing trade in the firm which became Scientific Roads Ltd. The partnership of Glossop and Hird seems to have worked uneventfully until the autumn of 1915 when a fire occurred causing severe damage. The interruption of work was a serious matter in itself but in addition the insurers of the York Gas Company sought to make Glossop and Hird personally responsible for the loss of the premises on the grounds, it would seem, that since their interest was not noted on the policy the insurer had a right of subrogation against them, notwithstanding that the Gas Company had undertaken to insure.[16] In fact this eventuality did not come to pass. Had it done so it would undoubtedly have ruined William Glossop for income was low because the volume of work available to tar-sprayers in 1915 was much reduced as the consequence of cuts in Local Authority spending and competition had become intense. He was convinced that two of his immediate competitors, Brothertons and Ellisons, from time to time, were cheapening the first cost of Tarvia they made by dropping the specification.[17] As has been noted the days of the pre-eminence of proprietary tars were coming to an end as more and more authorities took to specifying tars to Road Board specification, a process which was accelerated with the arrival of more exacting criteria in the post-war period 1919-26, dealt with in the next chapter. By 1915, W.& J. Glossop were already trading over a far larger area of the country than that contemplated in the 1907 agreement with Bristowe. In some ways this was a welcome development to the latter, in view of the confidence he obviously felt in dealing with Will Glossop, but it also involved him in protests from his licensees in other areas. This latter point was put to William during a visit to Hipperholme by Parker, one of Bristowe's lieutenants, and followed up in an official letter of January 14, 1916. It brought a very brisk reply, dated January 18, from William who said:

> As to tarspraying, when we entered into Tarspraying Contracts at first it was helpful to the sale of 'TARVIA' in our own district and it was our intention for several cogent reasons to confine ourselves principally to the North of England, but the advent of so many new, powerful tarspraying competitors and the competition of all the other important Tarspraying Contractors has made tarspraying in the North of England, generally and especially in the West Riding, valueless. When we tell you the prevailing price we had to contend with last year - 1½d per yard sweeping, spraying and gritting, including all labour and materials - you will understand that tarspraying in our district has not been desirable. We are therefore faced with the position of either taking undesirable contracts, going outside our own area, or giving up tarspraying altogether. You say you will not permit us to tender for spraying 'TARVIA' outside our own district. We presume you mean you would

not supply us with 'TARVIA' for any such contracts. It seems very strange that you should penalize us like this because we are your 'TARVIA' agents here, as it means we are not to have equal privileges with Contractors who may be nothing to you. Would it meet the situation if we were to run our tarspraying business under another name such as the National Road Tar Spraying Company?

The difference appears to have been resolved in Glossop's favour, probably by Fred Bristowe's personal intervention, as no more was heard of it.

Despite the volume of business being transacted William Glossop retained the management largely in his own hands, partly because there were few whom he trusted and partly for reasons of economy. The head office remained at his house, Highfield, Hipperholme, until he bought Amisfield House in October, 1923. The operation of the firm was carried on with an administrative and office staff of only five men,[18] four of whom subsequently became prominent in the firm's affairs. The longest serving was Harry Stephenson who joined in the Spring of 1906. Arthur Rideal was taken on in 1907 about the same time as William took Ralph Willsdon, the younger son of his sister Susannah, onto the staff to serve an unpaid 'apprenticeship' of three years, learning the trade. The fourth was Frank Willsdon, Ralph's elder brother, who came in 1914. Ralph Willsdon later managed the tar works, and Harry Stephenson was the estimator. In 1911 his salary was thirty shillings (£1.50) a week. Arthur Rideal received seventeen and sixpence (87½p) whilst Ralph Willsdon, in the first year he was paid at all, had only seven shillings (35p) a week. The survivors of the quartet - Harry Stephenson died in 1958 - recalled (in *Glossops are Sixty, 1906-1966*) how arduous it was to work for William Glossop. He drove himself without mercy and expected his young staff to do the same. A stock riposte to a request for a week's holiday was to wither the enquirer with a fierce glance and bark at him 'Why? Aren't you very well?' In fact they were usually given a week's holiday and a holiday sovereign which he invariably held on to until 1 o'clock on the Saturday afternoon, and salaries were increased, if at all, in increments of sixpence (2½p) per week.

Notwithstanding this outward tyranny towards them he must have held them in true and deep regard for he made them his partners in 1920 and, in due course, directors of the limited company which was formed in 1926 as will be seen in the next chapter.

[1] Letter 10.12.07 to Schibsted, the Norwegian manager of the Brooke brothers' Scandinavian quarry interests.

[2] Letter to Clarkson & Buckley, his solicitors, 13.11.06

[3] Partners' memo book, Amisfield House.

[4] Personal letter to the author 14.7.77

[5] Letter 27.10.06 to W.W. Canham, Bradford

[6] Letter 4.3.07 to J.C. Kerr, Manager of the Commercial Bank, Halifax

[7] Personal communication to the author by Mr. John Page 23.6.77

[8] *Doncaster Gazette* 3.7.08

[9] William Glossop's estimating note-book, Amisfield House

[10] *Halifax Evening Courier* 23.10.08

[11] Letter to Ernest Brown, Lightcliffe, 7.12.08, seeking his confirmation that he was a witness to the offending party having made derogatory comments: - one of several such letters.

[12] Letter to Lancashire & Yorkshire Railway 2.3.09

[13] Letter to H. Ellison, Surveyor of Taxes, Skipton, 10.11.09

[14] Letter from Glossop to Bristowe 18.2.1910

[15] Letter to Bristowe 25.7.11

[16] Letter to Spencer 2.12.15

[17] Letter to Bristowe 18.1.16

[18] Letter to Reserved Occupations Committee, Board of Trade 15.11.15

Fig.10. Surface dressing in the old style in the twenties with two hired rollers, hired horses and carts for grit distribution and, doubtless, another hired horse on the tar boiler which was probably the only piece of plant, apart from the wheelbarrow, in the picture that was owned by Glossops. The chargehand in the right foreground appears to be pouring tar into a pot-hole to grout in some stone filling.

Fig.11. A line of private owner railway wagons bearing the Glossop name and used for transporting crushed granite from the Close Quarry at Embleton.

Fig.12. A horse-drawn hand pumped tar boiler/sprayer of the type used in early surface dressing contracts.

Fig.13. (below left) Jim Fouracre with another early tar boiler/sprayer c.1909. He stayed with Glossops for the rest of his working life and eventually became branch manager at Grantham.

Fig.14. (below right) A more developed sprayer of 1927 with a paraffin engine to drive the pump and hand held spray nozzles.

Chapter 3

The Partnership

Whilst William Glossop, as narrated in the preceding chapter, had been gradually realigning the managerial situation within the firm, the external situation in which it found itself operating was very much changed from that which had prevailed before the conflict of 1914-18. Motor vehicles had undergone rapid development during the war and their numbers had increased at a dramatic rate. Whereas in March, 1910, the total of registered vehicles was 143877 by 1920 the total had risen to 650148.[1] More importantly, not only had the number of vehicles increased but the part they had played in the conduct of the war had improved their public image. From being something of a public ogre in 1910 the motor car driver graduated, if not to the status of public hero, at least to the point of his being regarded with tolerance or indulgence hence meriting more attention being paid to the road surfaces he drove upon. Furthermore, war-time events had demonstrated, both in remedial work done to roads behind the lines in Flanders and on the military traffic routes in the United Kingdom, that surface dressing was no mere dust palliative but had considerable value in increasing the life expectancy of road surfaces used by motor traffic. It is true that this doctrine had been preached pre-war by Henry Maybury, both when surveyor to the County of Kent and as chief engineer to the Road Board, but it was his war-time work at home and in France which gave added weight to his theories. Under his direction, for instance, the whole route from the military base at Aldershot to the war-time ferry terminal at Richborough near Sandwich had been tarred and gritted to save it from disintegration, in which objective he achieved marked success.

Though the war had highlighted the advantages of tar-spraying main traffic routes it had also produced a back-log of repairs to the general road system which had been subjected to an increase in traffic at a time when curtailment of public expenditure on civilian work and the loss of men to the forces had combined to cut back road maintenance. Whilst road authorities strove simultaneously to catch up on the back-log of repair and to carry out the essential improvements necessitated by the increase in the numbers of road vehicles the immediate post-war period saw, therefore, an upsurge in the volume of roadworks carried out both by the direct labour employed by road authorities and by contractors. This high demand made road plant, particularly rollers, expensive and coincided with a period of high demand for tar (or, more properly, the pitch that made up about two-thirds of the volume of distilled tar). Continental supplies of pitch, which was widely used in France and Germany for bonding coal dust and small coal into fuel briquettes, had been restricted by war damage in Belgium and Northern France and the post-war upheavals in the Ruhr, and consequently available supplies commanded high, though fluctuating, prices.

This latter factor made tar distilling a profitable trade for some four or five years after the war and also encouraged the use of refinery bitumen as an alternative surface dressing. However, despite the increased and increasing demand for tar and refined bitumen for surface dressing there was still insufficient appreciation of the importance of viscosity in determining the behavioural properties of tar and bitumen even though Hutchinson's invention of the tar viscometer had made measurement of viscosity possible. Whilst it is true that by the 1920s some of the more advanced councils and corporations specified viscosities, by contrast, until 1923 viscosity was not mentioned in the standard specifications for tar issued by the Ministry of Transport (into which the old Road Board had been merged). Even when viscosity was specified it was low - about 17 e.v.t. (using the modern equiviscous temperature system of expressing viscosity) - compared with modern surface dressings amongst which e.v.t. values are commonly in the fifties and sometimes in the sixties.[2] Low viscosities made tar very fluid when hot and hence easy to apply but injured the public image of tarred roads because of the ease with which low viscosity tars softened in hot, dry weather, causing them to relax their hold on the grit or chippings and promoting a greasiness in the surface which adhered to the tyres or led to skidding. Tar distilling, immediately post-1918, remained a relatively unsophisticated and fragmented industry.

So far as the new Glossop partnership was concerned an early decision after the war was to remove the tar distillery from the actual site of York Gas Works onto land leased from the Derwent Valley Light Railway at Osbaldwick on the south east outskirts of York. There is little doubt that so far as the senior partner was concerned the threatened claim against him over the fire rankled but, over and above this, the move had the practical value of increasing the firm's freedom in buying crude tar and enabled new plant to be installed. Ralph Willsdon moved to Osbaldwick as manager but, recognising that his own empirical knowledge of the technical and chemical aspects of the business was not adequate for the demands of the times, he appointed a young chemist, Ernest Milner (1899-1978), to be his assistant with responsibility for quality control and, nominally at least, research. Willsdon soon came to value Milner at least as much for his orderly thinking and general aptitude for business as for his knowledge of coal tar chemistry.

The new works came into operation in mid-year 1923 but its capacity was never equal to supplying the whole needs of the firm. Despite its limited capacity (about 6000 tons annually) it was a competently run works and enabled its owners to market their own branded tars - *Vitar* and *Super-Tar*. The firm always took the tar distillery seriously and, though modest in scope, it had sparked off an improved design of still, patented in 1921 (No.184242) which was deemed sufficiently important to be patented also in Canada, Australia, France, Italy, and South Africa. Although the warm friendship between Fred Bristowe and William Glossop continued until William's death in 1930 the old trading arrangement with Bristowe gradually withered away during this period with, as far as can be judged, no formal termination nor any disagreement with Fred Bristowe. Circumstances had changed, however. On the one hand making and selling machinery had become an important part of the Bristowe concern and Bristowe had developed commercially the low temperature distillation business which made *Coalite* smokeless fuel thus decreasing his interest in the branded tar market. On the other hand the importance of even the best branded tars, amongst which Tarvia must undoubtedly be included, was declining before the twin onslaughts of increased research and the acceptance of the standard specification for tars. In the early twenties, because of coal tar shortage and high demand, within the tar distilling trade itself, individual firms, as sellers, had not much to fear from each other but a good deal from the competition of the bitumen producers. As buyers, though, bidding against each other for crude tar supplies caused them considerable worries.

It was largely this, coupled with the bitumen threat, that encouraged the cooperative spirit which began to appear amongst tar distillers in the early twenties. Tentative at first and, in many cases, initially amounting to no more than an armed truce, as the Continental pitch market began to stabilise, and with the realisation of the commercial benefits likely to accrue both to producers and distillers of tar by combining into larger units, it developed along more formal lines. In the South Yorkshire area seven firms - namely Stainsby & Lyon Ltd. of Aire Tar Works, Knottingley; Major & Co. Ltd. of Hull; Bretherton & Co.Ltd. of Leeds Bridge, Leeds; Ellison & Mitchell Ltd. of Kilnhurst, Rotherham; Robinson Brothers Ltd. of Birmingham (who had works in Yorkshire); and Henry Ellison Ltd. of Cleckheaton - had associated in an area ring which, amongst themselves, was known as South Yorkshire Tar Distillers (SYTD). At first Glossops were not in this ring, an omission which seems to have caused some concern amongst the ring members.

Whilst Arthur Rideal was representing the firm at the Public Works Exhibition at the end of November, 1923, he 'happened' to be invited to lunch by Edgar Fellows of Midland Tar Distillers Ltd., Birmingham, the parent company of Robinson Brothers, and M. Mackintosh Williams, a director and leading shareholder of Walter H. Brown & Co. Ltd., the old established tar and chemical merchants of 4 Fenchurch Avenue, London E.C.3. Over lunch Fellows and Williams broached the possibility of Glossops, as distillers, joining the ring or, at least, coming to a trading agreement with it.[3] In beginning with Rideal the two negotiators had perhaps been deceived by his mild manner and disarming appearance into thinking he was a softer option than William Glossop. Although this was far from being the case he was certainly able to appreciate the danger to the tar distilling part of the business if a battle developed with the ring which had the capability of bidding Glossops out of their crude tar sources and of withholding their own supplies. Rideal reported to his partners on the matters discussed and William Glossop took over the negotiations.

Invited to meet Williams, whom SYTD had appointed as their negotiator, at Birmingham in mid-December he temporised, pleading illness and, in consequence, a first brief meeting took place at the Great Northern Hotel, Leeds, on January 3, 1924. As a result Glossops were offered a deal by which ring members would, firstly, refrain from out-bidding them for the York Gas Works crude tar and that from one or two small works from which they were currently taking tar and, secondly, to 'find ......not more than a further 1000 tons of crude tar annually'.[4] William Glossop waited a week and then replied in a temporising vein asking that the quantity of tar to be supplied be raised to 1500 or 2000 tons. Williams then had to go abroad until early April and, by a remarkable display of skilled procrastination, William Glossop drew out discussions for the rest of the year. Various points were threshed out during summer and autumn - the volume of tar that could be sold to Glossops, the basis of price per ton, the periods when delivery was to be made (SYTD wished to meet Glossops' demand for larger supplies of crude tar by deliveries in winter when the spraying department did not use it which meant putting down further storage tanks at Osbaldwick) - punctuated by Williams' absences. By the end of 1924 a draft agreement was in being but, at this critical point, William Glossop became ill, this time very seriously, and it was not until October 12, 1925, that the discussions were picked up again, though the parties, in the meantime, had more or less honoured the unsigned agreement. At the end of the year the partners involved Ralph Willsdon in the proceedings as well as William Glossop, by which time, however, SYTD were embarked upon negotiations aimed at amalgamating all the principal tar distillers of Yorkshire into one concern, and the idea was seeded of Glossops' tar distillery interests being merged into the new combine which was to be known as Yorkshire Tar Distillers Limited (YTD). How far William Glossop, with his fiercely competitive and individualistic outlook, ever became reconciled to his old adversaries such as Fred Ellison of H. Ellison & Sons is perhaps questionable but his less belligerent partners do not seem to have experienced difficulty in coming to terms with them.

Although the emergence of formal schemes for co-operation was not limited to Yorkshire, in this present history it is necessary to confine our attention to that area. By the end of 1925 the temporary excess of demand over supply in the pitch market in Western Europe had righted itself and in the resultant buyer's market the industry had begun to appreciate the benefits of concentration and co-operation. When YTD came into being in 1926 it amalgamated the tar distilling activities of eleven firms among whom were numbered W. & J. Glossop. Initially fourteen plants went into YTD and six more followed rather later. On the production side it took the tar output of sixty-nine gas works and sixteen coke-oven works.[5] The year 1926, therefore, marked the end of Glossop participation in tar distilling. Ralph Willsdon did not wish to go to YTD but returned instead to the main fold, and Ernest Milner, whom the partners counted too valuable to lose moved to head office at Hipperholme. Glossops took shares in YTD in satisfaction of the value of Osbaldwick Distillery. Although that part of the Osbaldwick site which housed the distillery passed to YTD, the remaining land at Osbaldwick was retained as a depot and as a site for the factory in which the firm made bitumen based paints - including their then well-known *Phlexo* bitumen based aluminium paint with which in one year they painted 5000 lamp posts in Kensington, London - and later the *Glossline* material used in their road marking activities.

The episode of the YTD negotiations brought the younger partners to the realisation that for all his powerful physique and apparently robust constitution William Glossop was not totally immune to serious illness and, in the more morbid sense, impressed upon them the fact of his eventual mortality. Furthermore, the younger partners had graduated into mature businessmen who saw the firm's future in the burgeoning trade in road surfacing and surface dressing in which, by the combined factors of Harry Stephenson's clever estimating and an enviable reputation for quality, they had become the leading firm in the country.

William, for his part, notwithstanding the energy and resource he consistently deployed into the road business, remained at heart a quarryman, deeply absorbed in that trade and all that it involved, an interest shared by Harry Stephenson who had been with him throughout the struggles concerning stone sources which had caused such anxiety in the firm's opening years. While William Glossop had seen the commercial sense of the YTD transaction and of the withdrawal of the firm from direct participation in distilling, stone quarrying was too close to his heart and to that of Harry Stephenson for it to be renounced. Though, as we have seen, the firm had divested itself of direct involvement in the troublesome ventures at Embleton and Horton, in 1921 it had acquired the Landemere Quarry at Northowram, Halifax, and in 1922 the Law Hill Quarry at Southowram, as well as, somewhat earlier, Yew Tree Quarry at Lightcliffe. Although these quarries, which produced Yorkshire stone mainly for steps, kerbs, and flags, with a secondary use for masonry purposes,[6] were of subsidiary importance in the firm's trading, the ownership and management of them was a source of great personal satisfaction.

It was, however, the road surfacing and surface dressing activities of the partnership which provided the bulk of the income and this saw the greatest developments in the twenties. The 'Tarviated' surfaces of Gladwell's system had run their course, water-bound macadam was in rapid decline - though as late as August, 1924, the firm quoted Thrapston Rural District Council for water-bound macadam, albeit to be top dressed immediately on laying with cold bitumen emulsion[7] - whilst in-situ grouting with tar, pitch, or bitumen was also fading rapidly despite a spirited attempt by several firms, including Allweather Mechanical Grouting, Mechanical Tarspraying & Grouting, Box Spraying & Grouting, and David Woods as contractors, and John Fowler as manufacturers of plant, to keep it alive. Glossops continued to quote for in-situ grouting when asked and, indeed, in April, 1924, secured a contract in Essex from Ongar Rural District Council for some 40 000 square yards of dry-laid granite grouted in-situ with Mexphalte. Their accepted estimate for laying 4" of granite, grouting with Mexphalte, rolling and surface dressing with Spramex (Shell-Mex's first essay into spraying grade bitumen), and chippings was 2s.7½d all in. Contracts for laying tarmacadam were more numerous and were executed mostly with site mixed material. Mixing in portable plants adjacent to the contract was in its heyday in the 1920s, regrettably often with indifferent results as many portable plants did not incorporate a dryer to dry the aggregate before coating.

It was surface dressing, however, that grew most rapidly in those first post-war years, partly in tar coating the remaining mileages of water-bound road but principally in recoating roads already tarred in previous years. Up to

26

1920 Glossops did their surface dressing with hand-pumped spraying machines (commonly known as 'man-killers') such as Bristowe's *Cantar* or, on small contracts, simply with tar boilers, cans and brooms though they had one machine described as 'an air pressure horse-drawn sprayer'[8], most likely an Aitken patent sprayer of the type used mainly by their competitors Taroads Ltd. Such machines as the Cantars were horse-drawn, though smaller boilers were moved manually, but Glossops never embarked upon horse ownership, preferring to hire from farmers or job-masters. The going rate for a horse c.1920 was about 3s.6d to 5s.0d per day.[9] In *Glossops are Sixty* Ralph Willsdon recalled that steady, patient horses were the most esteemed, an old barge-horse being ideal. Grit distribution was mostly done by hired horses and carts or hand-barrow, and final spreading was by hand. Before 1920 the only British firm who could be said to have made a commercial success of self-propelled tar sprayers were Taroads who used machines based on Aitken's patent, though in France the Lassailly distributor had some success as did the Saybolt and American Tar Company machines in the United States. The Taroads sprayers were mostly mounted on steam wagon chassis built by Mann's Patent Steam Cart & Wagon Company in Leeds. There had been no lack of experiment with bulk spraying equipment prior to 1914 though the cheapness of labour for hand spraying had not made it a pressing urgency. The shortage of men during the war and the sudden upturn in the volume of work available immediately after the war, coupled with higher wages and a generally shorter working day stirred up interest in machine spraying in the period 1918-20. Several of the established tar-boiler firms, such as William Weekes of Maidstone and Phoenix of Chard, began canvassing for orders for lorry or steam wagon mounted sprayers, whilst John Fowler & Co. in Leeds, in conjunction with the spraying firm of David Woods of Yeadon, commenced manufacture of a self contained spraying plant in which the actual steam roller carried the spray equipment, with tar stored in belly tanks beneath the boiler, and towed a grit hopper.

Having noted some of the shortcomings of the available proprietary equipment the Glossop partnership commissioned a steam wagon mounted sprayer, incorporating their own patented design, from Atkinson & Co. of Frenchwood Works, Preston. The basic idea of the Glossop nozzle was the discharge of two opposing tangential jets of tar from the nozzle body which were calculated to collide with each other and produce even dispersal into droplets. The density of application was regulated by the road speed of the spraying vehicle. In the hands of a skilful crew such vehicles were capable of producing a very workmanlike job and it was not until the modern Ashurst sprayers appeared in the early 1950s that a markedly better spray bar became available. Apart from contributing the basis of the design of the spraying apparatus Glossops appear to have been content to leave the development work to Atkinsons which, in practice, probably meant J. Sadler, their chief designer and co-patentee with Edward Atkinson of certain features of the Atkinson wagons. It is Sadler's signature that appears on surviving correspondence between Atkinsons and Glossops.

The new wagon was delivered by road to Hipperholme. Subsequently it was driven to York by Frank Birkett, a steam wagon driver who already worked for Glossops as a driver of the Foden and Clayton & Shuttleworth steam wagons they owned. Ralph Willsdon was its principal sponsor and it fell to him to arrange a well publicised demonstration on a stretch of roadway at Nunnery Lane in York on October 9, 1922. Frank Birkett drove the wagon, Walter Jones, the tar works foreman, was in charge of the spraying and another old retainer, Jim Fouracre, was the third man. Of the partners William Glossop, Arthur Rideal, and Harry Stephenson watched, so to speak, from the sidelines. The first wagon mounted sprayer and the similar wagons which were soon added to the fleet were referred to as 'automatic tar sprayers' or 'autars', references which did rather less than justice to the skill required on the part of the crew.

There is no doubt that the use of the self-propelling tarsprayers revolutionised the firm's turnover. The table on page 32 shows the areas of road sprayed from 1921 to 1928 inclusive matched with the number of tarsprayers in use during the respective seasons Notwithstanding intense competition, the area sprayed in 1928 was more than three times that carried in 1923 whilst the trading profit on surface dressing increased from £12 230 for the 1923 summer to £30 044 for the summer of 1927.[10] The scale of this tarspraying business really eclipsed the other activities of the firm.

Harry Stephenson had begun to emerge as a force as formidable as William himself. As the estimator he had had notable success in tendering for work for the London boroughs and in 1922[11] was despatched to London to open a permanent office at Sentinel House, Southampton Row, Bloomsbury. One of his early successes was with the Metropolitan Borough of Lewisham where he secured and held, against severe competition, a substantial though fluctuating annual yardage of work. In 1923 he carried out about one million square yards in Lewisham but by 1929 the area was down to about 850 000 square yards though it was up to over the million mark again in 1931 and 32 only to come down to just over 900 000 in 1933 as the economies inflicted by the slump began to bite.

By 1925, when the gross income from surface dressing alone topped the £100 000 mark, the firm had become a very large concern to be the subject of a simple partnership. The warning signals had been set by the long delays in the Yorkshire Tar Distillers negotiations brought about by William's protracted illness in the autumn and winter of 1924/25, and again in the autumn of 1925 even after making allowances for some degree of diplomatic indisposition. In 1926, therefore, the firm was reconstituted as a private limited liability company, W. & J. Glossop Limited, in which the shares were held by William Glossop, Harry Stephenson, the Willsdon brothers, and Arthur Rideal, all of whom were directors. Luke Bradley, a former school-master who had married Nellie Glossop, was company secretary. Ernest Milner, himself no believer in slack administration, recalled the latter as a particularly dour and humourless disciplinarian, addicted to trivial acts of oppression aimed principally at demonstrating the extent of his authority.[12]

There can be little doubt that in turning the business into a private limited company the younger partners, at least, were intent on avoiding, by intelligent anticipation, the complication and delay which would have occurred in the affairs of the firm on the death of a partner,[13] and equally, after the experiences of 1925, there cannot be much doubt that the partner looked upon as most vulnerable was William Glossop. Though only in his mid-fifties, in fact he was beginning to feel the effects of the strain imposed on him by the events of the ten years from 1906 to 1916 and the general stresses of the war and immediate post-war years. The fierce spirit which had carried him quickly to senior office in Brookes Ltd. and had sustained him through the initial decade of his own firm began to flag a little. There is no evidence, however, that his outlook mellowed at all. In 1922 he had a dispute with the Hipperholme Urban District Council over a piece of his land which they had taken for allotment gardens, and carried this as far as an appeal to the Ministry of Agriculture. He amused himself by going through all his personal papers, discovering amongst them a forgotten depositors pass book of the Yorkshire Penny Bank in Leeds into which he had paid £6.5s.0d in 1892 and a further £5 in 1896. He wrote to the bank in January, 1923, enquiring what his modest deposits and the accrued interest were then worth.[14] He also found that Clarksons, his solicitors in Leeds, had not returned the papers they had had when representing him in the lawsuits with Brookes Ltd. and they too received a tart letter.[15] He further managed to get into a dispute, which needed the services of a solicitor to resolve it, with the headmistress of the girls school to which he sent his nieces, Marjorie and Dorothy.

As the twenties advanced he gradually began to share control more effectively with his partners, particularly with Harry Stephenson, devoting his afternoons to those congenial aspects of his position that pressure of work had obliged him to forgo in earlier days. In fine weather he would sometimes motor over to the golf course to entertain clients; on other days he would explore the roads over the moors in his Bentley, of which marque he was a devotee,[16] or, on Saturday afternoons, he would watch the games of the Halifax Rugby League Club at Thrum Hall, Halifax. As a young man he had been a keen player and in his middle age supported the club by his personal and financial patronage. Probably the watershed in this process of handing over was his illness in 1925. The YTD negotiations were the last in which he took a solo major role.[17]

Because he allowed his partners a greater share of administration it is not, however, to be imagined that he was, in any real sense, a spent force. It was simply that, no longer an active player, he now managed the game from the touch line. His knowledge of likely processes of thought in a given road authority or its senior officers was invaluable for much could depend upon an accurate forecast of their reactions. A case which illustrates this point is that of Norfolk County Council with whom the company did a considerable volume of business in the mid and late twenties. The total area of spraying was about five million square yards for which tenderers had to state their price per thousand yards. The old hands among the firms tendering knew, however, that no one firm would get all of the work and that it would be divided, after a haggle, between the five or six lowest tenderers. There were seven divisions in the county and the work was mostly awarded on the basis of one contractor to each division, although sometimes one man took two divisions. Division W1, the Hunstanton area, containing miles of difficult and isolated rural roads was much less sought after than, say, E2 division (Norwich) and it was worth dropping the rate considerably to get E2 in preference to W1. Tenders for the 1925 season had to be in by November 17, 1924, and the six lowest tenderers were interviewed on December 22 by Major S.H. Warren, the then County Surveyor of Norfolk County Council. Glossops were offered W1 at their tendered price of £6.15s.0d per 1000 yards but by dropping the price by 2s.6d managed to secure instead the desired E2 area.[18] To be able to evaluate the relative characteristics of different divisions and by how much it was worth lowering the unit price to get one division in preference to another involved the deploying of a good deal of experience even in one county but the collective knowledge and experience required to tender for work of about twenty counties annually was prodigious, involving knowing not only the physical characteristics of the terrain and the availability of local materials, labour and cartage but also the personal foibles of the divisional engineers and their staffs. In all this, particularly in respect of the Midlands and the North, William was an invaluable repository of knowledge on which it was possible to build an ever widening experience of more distant counties. The probing further and further afield from Hipperholme sent the firm into Scotland where large programmes of road improvement were afoot in the twenties, most importantly from Glossops point of view, in surface dressing water-bound roads in rural areas and the Highlands, and eventually (post 1945) into the Republic of Ireland.

In 1930, whilst the firm was still in the midst of this surge of expansion and prosperity, William Glossop died at the age of sixty. On Saturday, February 8, he was in the office as usual, taking his part in all that was going on. Indeed a memo he wrote in his curious mixture of long and short hand was framed and preserved on the mantelpiece in the board room at Amisfield House. A little before one o'clock he went home to Highfield, lunched, and went out to watch a rugby match at Thrum Hall. After the game he collapsed in his car, was taken home unconscious, and died the next day, never having regained consciousness. In 1933 Emily, his widow, remarried, becoming Mrs. Cockcroft, and lived until 1964, narrowly missing her centenary.

By common consent Harry Stephenson stepped into the vacant chair. His commanding presence, his achievements in the preceding four or five years, including his success in initiating and promoting the London office, made him virtually an inevitable choice. Despite widespread regret at the passing of the old master - and most of the staff had worked under no other - the transition of captaincy of the company into the hands of Henry Stephenson was accomplished without visible upheavals. However, the threat that was appearing and growing larger week by week was that of the slump already apparent in the United States.

The firm had already weathered the General Strike and the prolonged miners' strike of 1926 both of which had had relatively little effect on it. The General Strike had occurred outside the spraying season but, in any case, the Glossop men were not, on the whole, union members. Although the coal strike had interfered with crude tar supplies by that time this circumstance constituted a problem for YTD rather than for Glossops in whose business any shortages of distilled road tar resulting from the strike were compensated for by increased use of refinery bitumen. Whilst the interests of road transport and the petroleum industry were much advanced by the strike those in the coal and coal related industries were heavy losers, both employers and employees.

Little more than a year after William Glossop's death the full effects of the slump hit the country and the resultant depression did not really begin to lift until 1935. During these four years there was a severe curtailing of expenditure on roads. Whereas in 1930 it had been near to £65½M, in 1935 it was only £51½M,[19] mostly achieved by a reduction in the scale of improvements. Surface dressing contractors, like undertakers, are less affected by recessions than many trades for the reason that making do with existing roads tends to promote maintenance at the expense of improvement. Nevertheless the firm did suffer some set-backs. The road area treated in 1933, for instance, was about 20½M square yards compared with 23M in 1930. In parallel with this altered pattern of road expenditure came changes in the trade itself. Insofar as the impact upon Glossops was concerned probably the most significant of these was the entry of the two major London gas companies into tar-spraying. The source of this initiative, begun in 1927, lay with Dr. Charles Carpenter, chairman of the South Metropolitan, after an exasperating journey down the Old Kent Road, London, to the company's works at Greenwich in the course of which his car became spattered with tar and chippings from carelessly executed tar-spraying. At the works he told his sales and technical staff to get into tar-spraying and to do it properly.[20] They did so to some purpose, with up-to-date sprayers mounted on Sentinel steam waggons, an example shortly to be followed by the Gas Light & Coke Co. and by Burt, Boulton & Hayward Ltd handling the tar output of a number of smaller gas companies. The law under which the gas companies operated precluded their doing more than spray the tar, this being deemed to be 'delivery'. The sweeping, gritting, and rolling had to be done by others, often local authority direct labour. This onslaught cut into the trading profits of the four major tar-spraying firms and, being confined mostly to the South of England, made competition very keen for the work tendered for by Harry Stephenson's London office. The fact that the trading stood up so well to it was a great credit to the thrift with which the London operations were conducted. Closely controlled though costs already were the combination of this enhanced competition with the arrival of the slump inevitably provoked further tightening of pressure on costs and a number of further economies were instituted. After Luke Bradley's death in September, 1930, Arthur Rideal acted as secretary as well as a director, with assistance from Ernest Milner, instead of a new company secretary being appointed. Amisfield House was considered something of an extravagance and was let at a rent of £100 a year to a local doctor from November 1, 1932, whilst for twelve shillings a week the firm rented back from Mrs. Glossop the offices it had used in the outhouses of Highfield before the move to Amisfield House. To some extent, however, this latter move was a reflection of company politics rather than of pure economics for the reason that the new chairman lived in London, ran the London office, and desired to see London become the operations centre of the company - an aspiration not shared by his fellow directors.

The nett profit for the eight years up to January 31, 1935, were:

Year ending January 31, 1928	£35 001
Year ending January 31, 1929	£32 808
Year ending January 31, 1930	£37 904
Year ending January 31, 1931	£32 193
Year ending January 31, 1932	£29 306
Year ending January 31, 1933	£24 579
Year ending January 31, 1934	£35 466
Year ending January 31, 1935	£32 026

It can thus be said that the company survived its trial fairly well. Other firms in the trade were not so fortunate. To quote an example, H.V. Smith & Co. Ltd. who had paid a 25% dividend in 1923-25 made losses in 1932 -34. The year 1931, when the Slump was at its nadir, saw the end of Fothergill & Sons Ltd., who had done a considerable area of tar-spraying in South Wales and the West of England. F.W. Elston, who had been supervisor for Fothergills in Exeter and Devon, having decided not to sink without a struggle, telephoned Harry Stephenson in London and put a proposition to him. He said that he was certain that he could tender a price that would secure the work of Exeter Corporation (about 133 000 square yards) and at which he could earn the company a profit. Stephenson went to Exeter, met him, liked him, and took him on, the only contract of service being a handshake as Stephenson caught the train at Exeter on his way home.[21] The association endured and Elston served the company as a manager and, later, a director, until he retired in 1963. Like the other directors he had learned his trade in a hard school and knew how to make pennies count. Stephenson treated the West of England trading as an adjunct of the London office, with Elston answerable to him rather than directly to head office. At first Elston conducted the firm's business from his own home, using his sitting room as an office and spending his Sunday evenings typing the firm's letters on his own typewriter. Later, in 1936, a one room office was secured in Queen Street, Exeter, and three years later a larger one (with a yard at the rear) over a barber's shop in Cowick Street. It was not until 1954 that a move was made finally into proper office premises on the new Pinhoe Trading Estate on the outskirts of Exeter.

The unhappy fate of the Fothergill firm was an extreme case of the malaise affecting the whole surface dressing trade. Many men who had been foremen or supervisors for the larger firms had found it relatively easy in the fat post-war years to set up in business in tar-spraying on their own account, and as competition had sharpened they had reduced the rates they tendered lower and lower until by the time of the Slump these were often suicidal. Small firms went mostly for the work of the many hundreds of lesser road authorities, County Councils on the whole preferring the larger firms. Though, as already explained, county work might be tendered for by some six or eight major contractors, submitting the lowest tender was not the end of the matter for, as with Norfolk County Council, it did not automatically secure the whole of the work. Instead it often merely initiated further bargaining with the two or three lowest tenderers, all of whom in the end might get a share of the work at unit prices approximating to the lowest tendered rate. In attempting to make a profit or, at least, avoid losses as a result of these very low prices there was the ever present temptation to cut corners in the execution, usually by increasing the yardage per gallon or by skimping on the sweeping, the quantity of grit, and the rolling. These practices earned the tar-spraying industry a bad name in the latter twenties, and those who did not deserve blame received as much of it as those who did.

Several of the firms combined to form the Association of Road Surface Dressing Contractors initially - or ostensibly - set up to promote higher standards of technique and workmanship but soon used as a medium for the exchange of tendering information and the securing of rates above suicidal level. By co-operating with the British Road Tar Association and the then newly formed Road Research Laboratory the Surface Dressing Association improved the technical standards of the industry and improved its public image. There was nothing illegal nor even immoral about the exchange of price information amongst members and, as in the case of the Road Rollers Association, formed in similar circumstances, the scheme was operated with good sense and discretion. Excessive profit margins would have defeated its objectives by driving employing authorities to direct labour. Probably the most significant technical advance promoted, in the late thirties, through the co-operation of these three bodies was the incorporating of a small percentage of stearine-amine and other wetting agents into surface dressing binder to promote adhesion and reduce the effect of a damp base surface upon the dressing.

The company continued to be interested in winning and working stone. Early in the 1930s the enclosing walls of North Castle, York, were demolished and Glossops purchased a quantity of the largest pieces of masonry which were carted to the Lightcliffe quarry for storage pending re-use.[22] Some were reworked for the construction of Spital Bridge over the York to Scarborough railway while further quantities were similarly used in the steps and landing of the pedestrian approaches to the new Lambeth Bridge in London, opened in July, 1932. In addition to these steps and landing Glossops also supplied the Elland Edge flags, with which the footways of the bridge were surfaced, from their quarry at Law Hill, Southowram, reputed to be one of the best veins of paviour's stone in West Yorkshire. Gratifying though the work on Lambeth Bridge must have been from the point of view of prestige the general quarrying activities were very firmly in second place to surface dressing, as were public works contracting and water main cleaning, the other activities of the company in the thirties.

The water main cleaning arose from William Glossop's shareholding, along with his friend Charles Sheard and others, in a concern known as the British Water Main & Sewer Cleaning Company whose activities centred around a patent for cleaning obstructed or encrusted underground mains by means of a rotary cutter fed up the pipe and powered through a long flexible shaft by a small petrol engine. By the end of 1930, after some quarter of a century of trading, the company was in low water and such assets as it still possessed were offered to and accepted by Glossops in July, 1931, for £50.[23] Glossops revived the business and continued to operate the process for another thirty years.

Although Glossops were then yet to feel the full effects of the Slump and were in a favourable trading position, they may still have had premonitions of what was to come. Hence diversification was in the board room air in the autumn of 1930. In November that year Harry Stephenson reported to the board that the company had been offered 12 000 square feet of factory floor area in 1¼ acres of ground at Park Royal, North London, for £4 500 and that it would be suitable for re-housing the London works, then at Chelsea Basin.[24] He was authorised to negotiate with the vendor and as a result it became Glossop property. The London depot was moved to Park Royal early in 1931 [25] but the property was, of course, far larger than was needed for a London depot and there was much surplus space.

Harry Stephenson had a heavy personal leaning toward London. Left to himself there can be little doubt that he would have abandoned Hipperholme as headquarters. The move from Amisfield House back to the outbuildings at Highfield may be considered as one manifestation of his preferences, which were given further weight by his moving the venue of a proportion of board meetings from Hipperholme to the Midland Hotel, St. Pancras. It is logical, though unprovable, to suppose that he would have liked to have used Park Royal as a head office and central works for the whole group. In this he failed to have his way. There were, however, other proposals for Park Royal including the making of the patent 'Lock and Lift' manhole cover, the rights of which had been offered to them by the patentee, and the manufacture of plant for glass bottle making. In both of these Stephenson ran into more board room opposition than he may have expected, the directors at the June, 1931[26] board meeting deciding to delay action on both proposals. The 'Lock and Lift' man, taking the hint, sold his patent elsewhere and the glass bottle machine project simply withered away. It was finally buried early in 1934 when, except for one sixth of an acre kept as a depot, the Park Royal site was sold for £6 000, having been bought three years before for £4 500, thus securing a profit of £1 500 and a free site.[27]

[1] Basic Road Statistics (British Road Federation)

[2] See G.H. Fuidge's authorative paper *The Viscosity of Tar - its Significance in the Surfacing of Roads*. Journal of the Society of the Chemical Industry Vol. LV (1936) pp301 -9

[3] File *Yorkshire Tar Distillers* - Amisfield House

[4] Letter from Macintosh Williams to Glossops 12.2.24

[5] J.B. Earle: *Black Top* (1974) Chapter 3.

[6] File of plans and documents relating to these three quarries (Amisfield House)

[7] Estimating book for 1923, 1924, and 1925 (Amisfield House)

[8] Register of plant, 1920, Amisfield House.

[9] Estimator's book, Amisfield House.

[10] File of annual analyses - Amisfield House

[11] Letter No.520 in William Glossop's personal letter book.

[12] Personal communication to the author 17.7.77

[13] Letter to S.J. Reading, General Manager of the Derwent Valley Light Railway. 28.1.27

[14] Letter No. 535 in William Glossop's personal letter book.

[15] Letter No.536 ibid.

[16] Letter No. 592 (and others) to Central Garage Ltd. ibid.

[17] Personal communication from Ernest Milner to the author 17.7.77

[18] Notes in Estimator's book 1924/25

[19] Basic Road Statistics (British Road Federation)

[20] J.B.F. Earle *Black Top* pp.198 and 199

[21] Related in a letter from Elston to Arthur Rideal 2.6.58 (Amisfield House)

[22] R.W. Willsdon *Glossops are Sixty*

[23] Minutes of board meeting 2.6.31

[24] Minutes of board meeting 4.11.30 and 2.12.30

[25] Minutes of board meeting 17.2.31

[26] Minutes of board meeting 2.6.31

[27] Minutes of board meeting 13.3.34

TABLE SHOWING AREAS SPRAYED 1921 - 28 inclusive.

SEASON	AREA SPRAYED	INCOME	FIRMS PROFIT for YEAR	STEAM SPRAYERS
1921	5 404 227 sq. yards	£78 852	£14 217	0
1922	6 771 083 sq. yards	£63 247	£ 8 762	1
1923	7 455 220 sq. yards	£74 400	£12 231	2
1924	10 213 988 sq. yards	£93 733	£19 165	7
1925	12 685 115 sq. yards	£102 672	£19 474	8
1926	15 093 452 sq. yards	£125 850	£19 812	8
1927	17 702 371 sq. yards	£175 909	£30 044	9
1928	22 667 043 sq. yards	£189 870	not available	11

Fig.15. Wallis & Steevens Simplicity *roller No.7832, the maker's prototype delivered new to E.Parry & Co. of Putney, London, in January, 1926, and bought by Glossops in 1938 for use at Exeter. It was single speed and could not be taken out of gear. The combined smokebox, forecarriage head and chimney base casting was unique to this engine. Later Simplicities had a revised design.* [James Gilbey collection]

Fig.16. *Sprayer No.101, the first of the series, with its driver, Frank Birkett (left). No.101 was the only wagon bought new with maker's standard water tank. Later purchases had a larger tank, up to cab roof height, and an extended coal bunker behind the cab.*

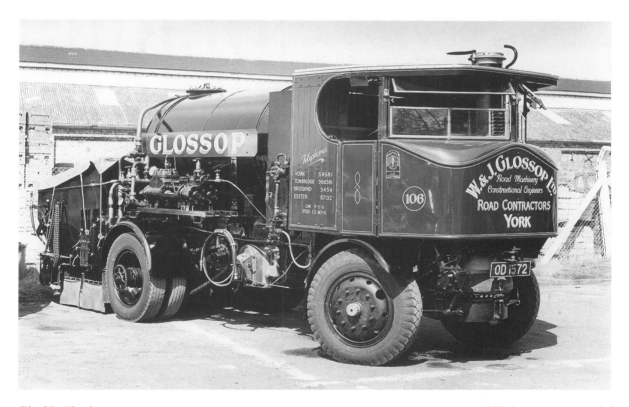

Fig.17. The last steam sprayer to be owned by the firm was their No.106 new in 1932 but not acquired by Glossops until 1952. Originally a DG4 tipper it came out new on pneumatics. Its real works number was 8666 but subsequently it carried the plate of Sentinel No.6400. It was completely reconditioned as a combination sprayer and gritter by Leon Birkett and his works staff at Hipperholme but when completed was lettered as belonging to the York office whose depot was at Osbaldwick. Soon afterwards the Hipperholme works was closed and all its functions were transferred to Osbaldwick. Later the wagon lived for a while at the Tonbridge depot but is now owned by David Coppard. [Bob Payne]

Figs. 18 and 19.
Two views of the Osbaldwick tar distillery under construction showing (top) the Benzole House framework and (lower) a northward looking view along the railway. These were taken by Luke Bradley, husband of William Glossop's sister, Nellie, and, later, company secretary. They were dated June 26, 1922.

Fig.20. The bulk of the output from the new distillery continued to be applied with hand pumped machines, most of which were Bristowe's Cantars as shown here. Compared with the steam wagon mounted sprayers they were achingly slow and incredibly hard work. This is obviously a demonstration but the site and purpose are not recorded.

Fig.21. In the original design for sprayers Nos.104 and 105 the arrangement was varied to suit bitumen, with the chassis longer and the directly heated tank moved closer to the rear. In this picture, date stamped January 7, 1924, a Westinghouse steam driven compressor is fitted on the centre of the chassis but this was not used in the wagons as delivered, the usual large water tank being then fitted behind the bunker with a smaller supplementary tank where the compressor was (see Chapter 7).

Fig.22. Nearside view of No.104 taken May 14, 1924, showing it as delivered.

Fig.23. Offside view of its sister engine No.105 taken May 28, 1924.

Fig.24. The early steam sprayers had a davit for hoisting barrelled tar to the tank top and a patented manhole with casters to allow the barrel to be rotated. However bulk delivery by road tanker commenced with No.121 (Atkinson No.294) shown new here in the depot at Hipperholme on April 8, 1924, together with its purpose built trailer.

Fig.25. The only known picture, taken in 1923, of the tarmac plant at Chelsea Basin, London, powered by Wallis & Steevens traction engine No.7456. In the background is one of the 5 ton Foden wagons.

Fig.26. Sprayer No.102 (Atkinson No.388) on March 29, 1922, soon after arrival at Hipperholme.

Fig.27. Fowler 15 ton roller No.9703, caught by the late Jack Wilkinson at the Hopgrove Inn near York, July 4, 1939. [Road Roller Association Archive collection].

Fig.28. The partners were delighted when in the early days of the limited company Harry Stephenson secured the contract to tarspray the roadway in front of Buckingham Palace. Here sprayer No.103 is seen with the Victoria Memorial on the left and Constitution Hill on the right of the picture.

Fig.29. A second view of the same job with No.103 in front of the main gates of the Palace.

Fig.30. Rear-end view of No.102 (Atkinson No.388) spraying. The man on the spraying platform could be seen by the driver in his rearview mirror. The situation is not recorded.

Fig.31. Even in a firm as deeply committed to steam as Glossops, by the late thirties the motor vehicle had begun to appear. The lack of steam for heating caused tank insulation to be taken more seriously as is evident from this 1940s' picture of a sprayer mounted on a second-hand Morris Commercial Leader chassis.

Fig.32. When this sprayer on a Bedford OY chassis, based on the London depot, was put into service in Spring, 1942, the sheet metal cleading enabled glass-fibre insulation to be used.

Chapter 4

From Private to Public

Buying out William Glossop's share of the business had taxed the resources of the surviving directors heavily and though they were the possessors of a sound and fairly profitable undertaking their available personal liquidity and, in some case, borrowing powers, were committed to the hilt. Whilst the Slump was at its worst and financial confidence at a low ebb it clearly would not have been sound policy to go public but when the worst effects of the depression began to ease off in 1934 the thought of turning the firm from a private to a public company, with the concomitant prospect of unlocking some of their personal capital from its embrace, began to appear increasingly attractive. Who first began to canvass the proposal is uncertain. Mr. Geoffrey Willsdon believed that his father, Frank Willsdon, and Uncle Ralph were early protagonists[1] but certainly by December, 1934, the Board was unanimous in a desire to investigate the possibilities.[2] Even at their lowest, the year ending January 31, 1932, profits had not fallen below £24 500, and two years later had recovered to over £32 000. Nevertheless, on the advice of their auditor, E.R.C. Kerr of Halifax, who acted for the firm from William Glossop's earliest days, and their brokers (Allison & Coulson of Newcastle upon Tyne) the directors offered 60 000 6% Cumulative Preference Shares of £1 each at twenty-one shillings each, payable in full on application. The new company was registered on April 18, 1935, with a capital of £120 000made up of the 60 000 preference shares just described and 120 000 ten shilling ordinaries issued to the owners of the old company as vendors. The preference shares were offered on May 29, 1935, and were well received. Though the sums involved may appear trifling by comparison with many current transactions in the capital market it is worth remembering that the nett profit of such an old and celebrated firm as Val de Travers Asphalte in the year 1934 was a mere £8 315, a little more than sufficient to meet the interest on the Debentures, whilst, as previously noted, one of their competitors, H.V. Smith & Co. Ltd., was turning in actual losses during the same period but somehow survived.

The firm had done well, therefore, and went on to do better in the next four years as the country eased away from the recession. In quarrying things went reasonably well. To retrogress slightly it should be mentioned that early in 1931 the board had commissioned a consultant geologist's report from Messrs. Yorkson & Fox on the quality of the untapped areas of stone at their Law Hill quarry and as a result of a very favourable report had decided to work the stone by sinking a new shaft,[3] the site being deemed unsuitable for open working. Initially the shaft sinking work was let out to a contractor on piece work but because of a slip in the measurements taken by Glossop's supervisor, Charles Naylor, the sub-contractor was overpaid £15 on account, which was corrected in the next payment, whereupon he refused to continue and abandoned the work.[4] After a short pause the sinking was resumed by direct labour and despite trouble from the heavy rainfall in August, 1931, the flag rock was bared in the first week of September. Law Hill, which was equipped with pneumatic tools supplied with compressed air from a modern electrically driven plant,[5] was an exceptional working in other ways. Not only was the stone won from it of the highest quality but the depth of workable stone was never less than 35 yards and at its deepest 40 yards in thickness.[6] As a kind of bonus the overlying shale was found to make good bricks, as was established by a trial batch made from it by Birkby & Son at Wyke Brickworks, near Bradford - actually two batches had to be made as the first was accidently sent away by the brickmakers with a load of their regular product[7] - but because the economic prospects of brickmaking were poor the idea of making bricks was eventually not pursued.[8]

However the overall market in York stone was shrinking, in part from the effects of the depression itself but mainly because cheaper but still acceptable substitutes in the form of hydraulically pressed concrete were available so that, even with the advantage of a top grade stratum of rock and a well equipped new quarry, the financial rewards were not high. Nevertheless quarrying was deeply embedded in the collective Glossop psyche, particularly in that of the chairman, and the ability to supply very high quality York stone paving, steps and copings from their own quarry probably yielded rewards not measurable in purely financial terms. To have pride in producing materials of superb quality is not an ignoble trait and if its achievement involved some sacrifice of financial advantage it must be remembered that the preference shareholders were protected against vicissitudes by their guaranteed dividend, whilst virtually all the other shares were owned by the board members and their families. Therefore, so long as they protected the preference shares, the board were justified in feeling at liberty to deploy the company's efforts in this way.

Whether or not, viewed from more than sixty years on, the investment at Law Hill could have earned a little more if used in other activities there is little doubt that in the four years following the formation of the public company it was conducted in a prudent and profitable manner. Surface dressing remained the firm basis of its trading but road surfacing had an important secondary position and the company moved increasingly into general public works contracting - road widening, kerbing, culverts, earthworks, drainage, and sewering. Work in estate roads, both for local authorities and private developers, formed an important element of these public works, as also did work under the Private Street Works Act, especially at the Exeter branch.

In all these developments and in the management methods themselves the controlling persona of Henry Stephenson loomed very large. Not for nothing had the formative period of his working life been spent in the shadow of the close grained and abrasive personality of William Glossop in the years of desperate struggle before 1914. As the years of his chairmanship went by he wrapped himself ever more closely in the mantle once worn by his deceased mentor. In short, he became more autocratic. He produced such successful results, however, that his fellow directors who, because of the extent of their shareholdings, had the collective power to have pulled him down had they so wished, never considered doing so even when most irked by the characteristics of his regime. Their personal regard for him and, it must be allowed, in some degree, the awe in which they held him contributed to this, though events toward the end of his reign brought revolt dangerously close. The strength and paradoxically the weakness of the board at that time was that Stephenson, so far as the other founder members were concerned, had always been top dog of the pack. He had been there when they came to the firm, had been William Glossop's right-hand man, had steered the company in the right course in many cases of perplexity, and had been the designer and co-ordinator of the immense expansion of the surface dressing trade. Hence, almost as the natural order of things, they allowed him the prerogative of final decisions.

He built up a management structure that reinforced this emphasis on personal authority, organising the firm's operations into geographical areas, each headed by a director or senior manager, with the management of each geared to an annual bonus system based upon the profits it earned. Neither the area managers nor area directors were outside this linking of salary to results, and additionally they had the forbidding task of being interviewed by him to explain any lapse in the level of output or profitability. This encouraged personal endeavour and collective thrift but increasingly made board members semi-strangers to each other by channelling communication through the chairman and his office. The executive staff were expected to and, indeed, did subordinate their whole life style to the requirements of the firm. Annual holidays consisted of one week only, and that restricted to the period outside the surface dressing season. William Holbrow recalled that when he joined the company in 1947 this was the proposition put to him, and that by standing out for two weeks annual holiday he became the first to enjoy a privilege which soon had to be extended to the rest of the staff.[9] The combination of the carrot and the stick worked in its time. Staff were very loyal and esprit de corp was good. Even in times of exasperation they managed to wring a laugh from their problems because the personal involvement of the board members with the staff was so close that in individual branches everyone knew everyone else from top to bottom. Consequently upon the Stephenson scheme of management the year 1939 found the firm in a highly effective condition - the members of the board, in their fifties, at the peak of their powers and experienced in their trade from its very beginnings; the staff and key workmen deeply versed in the effective execution of work; and the plant equal to or better than any in the United Kingdom.

By the late thirties the company's operations were consuming a considerable, if fluctuating tonnage, of coated macadam for road surfacing, all of which had to be purchased from outside makers. Henry Stephenson and the board perceived, in advance of many of their contemporaries, that large-scale tarmacadam trading in the future would depend upon possession of a sound aggregate source where it would be possible to combine the quarrying of the necessary bulk stone with the operations of crushing, grading, drying and coating, and where, at the same time, rail facilities would exist for shipping coated stone to what J.B. Earle has called ' the roadstone deficiency area' of London and the South East where virtually the only locally quarried roadstone is the hard-won Kentish rag. All this sound assessment was marred in the execution by the first example of what was, in the next dozen years, increasingly to flaw Stephenson's commercial judgement, namely put colloquially 'spoiling the ship for a ha'porth of tar'. Hartshead Quarry at Hartington, Derbyshire, the limestone source eventually selected in 1937, was not quite good enough either in quality and disposition of the stone or in situation in relation to consumers to fulfil what was required of it and the consideration that it was cheap in capital cost seems to have overridden a dispassionate evaluation of these operational disadvantages that, in the end, were to bring about its downfall. Hartshead had plenty of good stone in it but only a limited quantity that could be won readily. Once this had been worked out its owners would face either the high expense of tapping further supplies or the risk of using inferior stone. This, however, lay in the future. For the time being it is sufficient to note the purchase of the quarry and the hiving off of the enterprise as a separate entity, Hartshead Quarries, which contributed coated macadam to the parent company's Midland area operations and supplied a number of outside customers, besides doing a certain amount of contracting in its own right.

The purchase of the quarry, however, was soon overshadowed by the outbreak of war in 1939. So far as company activities were concerned it did not call for any collective heroic feats - though many Glossop people subsequently served in the Forces with distinction and bravery. The 1939 spraying season was all but over and the various contracts came to their conclusion without incident. However there were some tasks out of the usual routine. For instance the York office received from the War Department a request and a contract at short notice to sand-bag the York hospitals and the War Department offices in the city, which housed Northern Command.

Another activity of that first autumn and winter of the war - the so-called 'phoney war' during which Germany digested Poland and not much else seemed to happen - was a very large amount of camouflage painting, particularly of runways and aircraft hangars. Later the firm built many airfield runways in preparation for the bomber offensive against Germany and undertook maintenance to many more. Though the scale of surface dressing of roads declined during the war years the amount done on airfields did more than compensate for it. Some of this work on bomber runways was carried out using a mixture of wood chippings and pulverised rubber in an effort to reduce the destructive abrasion of bomber tyres without sacrificing the grip of the tyres on the treated surface.

Hipperholme depot produced a large low-loader trailer hauled by a Sentinel tractor for moving plant onto and off airfields. Transporting plant by low-loader became commonplace within ten years but until the early war years few firms did it. For instance, the Eddison Steam Rolling Co. Ltd., from whom Glossops hired many of the rollers they used, did not own a low-loader until after it became a part of the Barford empire in 1947, and rollers travelled long distances under their own power. The Glossop machine did many extended journeys and its crew displayed great tenacity and resource in moving urgently needed plant from job to job and in moving broken-down machinery to a place of repair, hampered by lack of sign posting by day and black-out by night. A steam wagon after dark was a difficult thing to make conform to the black-out. The glare from the firing chute during firing-up was alone sufficient to make its presence obvious, whilst if the wagon was hard worked flames could easily appear at the chimney top, particularly when burning soft coal.

After the fall of France in 1940 there came the added hazard of enemy bombing attacks, at first the daylight raids of the Battle of Britain period but soon followed by the night onslaughts upon London and many of the major cities of the country, which began in the autumn of 1940 and continued far into 1941. In common with most civil engineering and road making contractors Glossops played their part in repairing air raid damage, both civil and military, but the greater part of their war work was on runway construction and maintenance and work in camps and munitions factories. One of the aerodrome contracts in which Glossops had a leading part was the upgrading in 1942 of the civil airport at Exeter for military use. By 1942 other parts of the airfield programme were largely completed but there was a further surge of activity in preparation for the invasion of France in 1944, during which Glossops undertook extensions at Yeovilton air base, but after this Glossops war effort came virtually to an end and the fall off of work continued into the immediate post-war months.

After the end of hostilities new construction work remained at a low ebb though surface dressing and resurfacing contracts picked up somewhat with the resumption of road maintenance which had fallen into arrears during the war. It was not long before the post-war housing drive was launched - at first in the programme of temporary housing which developed from the emergency hutting erected in 'flying bomb' areas whilst the war was still on, but soon afterwards in more developed schemes of permanent housing, both traditional and system-built. Most such developments involved building new roads and sewers and the share of these works which Glossops were able to secure gave a useful fillip to the trading figures. The Exeter office was able, for instance to pick up several such jobs for Exeter Corporation, none large but all useful to have. The earliest of these came only a few months after the end of the war when there were many thousands of Germans still in prisoner-of-war camps and, because of the shortage of civil engineering trade labour, F.W. Elston, who was in charge of Exeter, applied for and obtained the services of a party of these prisoners. W.D. (Bill) Binnie, later the director in charge of the South Western office, went down on the first morning with Charlie Bond, who was to be the foreman, taking with them a lorry load of plant and site huts. Charlie was a foreman of the old school, and a Devon man to boot, witty, resourceful and ingenious, but to be confronted, as he shortly was, with a bus load of hefty and mildly hostile young men all speaking a language of which he knew nothing, dismayed even him. However, Bill Binnie, who was also somewhat puzzled as to how Charlie would cope, took care to conceal his own doubts and encouraged him by counselling him to look for a prisoner who spoke a little English and make him the ganger man. By about eleven o'clock on the same day he revisited the site to find Charlie all smiles, the huts up, the plant unloaded and work begun. The old man gave him a nudge in the ribs. 'We're going to be alright' he said, 'Got one here who speaks English. I think he must have been to Cambridge - he's got a Cockney accent'.

The tarspraying plant in use at that period was not radically different in concept to that introduced some twenty years before but so far as wagon mounted sprayers were concerned had undergone a process of continuous improvements of detail. Of these the most noticeable was the introduction of cylindrical tanks instead of the rectangular type used in the original series of Atkinson sprayers. The first spraying machines thus equipped were two Yorkshire steam wagons (see Chapter 7) which before being bought by Glossops had been owned by Shell Mex. These had cylindrical tanks when purchased and were fitted with heater coils that ran longitudinally through the tank at low level. Not only did cylindrical tanks suffer less from the stress cracking induced by chassis flexing but also emptied better whilst the altered arrangement of the steam coils improved the heating capacity. Other changes brought in included making each jet controllable by its own system of operating levers and rods, thereby facilitating width adjustment and the fitting of an integral grit box and distributor on the back of the wagon chassis. An alternative to this was the use of the two wheeled Bunce towed gritter (manufactured by William Bunce & Sons of Ashbury, near Swindon).

Spraying was destined to be the last commercial employment of steam vehicles and, so far as capital cost was concerned, it was economical to use steam wagons for it was possible to buy a sound chassis, overhaul it, paint it, and get it on the road for not much more than £150. Nevertheless there were compensating disadvantages. To maintain the constant speed necessary for good surface dressing required a skilled driver and it was essential to ensure that no water drips or spillages whatever fell on to the surface being coated. In order to raise steam before work could begin the driver of a steamer had to be prepared to rise an hour or an hour and a half before the rest of the gang, and had to clinker off the fire and bank down at night. He had to wash out the boiler about once a week, hump coal into the bunker, pick up water at fairly frequent intervals from roadside supplies, oil up the engine each morning and check over glands and joints for tightness. Such routines were all but second nature to the older drivers but as the need for younger men occurred such rigours were much less acceptable. Men who when they were in the forces had driven petrol or diesel vehicles with self starters and single point lubrication were not terribly interested in taking on a steam wagon which required this degree of attention. From being able to choose the best from a line of applicants as they had in pre-war days, the plant managers found they had to take on any tolerably qualified candidate who presented himself.

Having to make do with drivers thus recruited combined with post-war shortages of materials and components - which led to a good deal of cobbling and making do - reduced the standards of condition of spraying machines, particularly in the London area where competition of other industries for labour was most acute. Fresh spraying machines were put on the road but how far they were new was problematical. As Arthur Rideal put it in a despairing moment in a letter to Elston they were 'built by us from odds and ends'.[10] This was an over-statement for the purpose of emphasis but it came at a time when the London tar-spraying section had had a very rough season because of plant trouble.

As ever, the truth lay with neither extreme of opinion. These post-war Glossop machines made in the works at Hipperholme were by no means put together from odds and ends but a major component, the carrying vehicle was second-hand and moreover used a prime mover - steam - associated in the popular eye, however unjustly, with obsolescence. In its time the Glossop spray equipment had equalled the best of its rivals and excelled many. The time had arrived, however, when something superior was available. The new Ashurst spray bar, introduced in 1949 by Grant, Galloway & Gear Ltd. of Ashurst, Southampton, incorporated a square hollow section spray bar with the combined swirl chambers, valves and spray nozzles entirely within it - bedded metal to metal with two planed surfaces in contact, enabling a high standard of accuracy to be achieved in manufacture and working with an ease that had not been approached hitherto. Within a few years this type of spray bar virtually captured the market but when it first appeared, instead of welcoming it as did many of his competitors, Harry Stephenson unfortunately reacted with a condemnatory letter to the trade press and a personal attitude which for some years inhibited its adoption by Glossops.

The general immediate post-war trend, however, was good. In 1947 the company secured a surface dressing contract from the County Council of County Dublin. Road work in the Republic of Ireland, both maintenance and improvement, had been kept at minimal volume for years because of the chronically low financial yields of local taxation, and the situation had been made bleaker by the lack of imported supplies and the general deterioration of the country's trade brought about by the war in which it was neutral. In retrospect the post-war road programme can be seen as one of the first steps in the process of economic betterment brought about by successive Irish administrations in the last fifty years. To carry out their contract Glossops sent a motor sprayer, the first non-steam outfit they had put on the road, consisting of an American made Etnyre spraying system, bought from the War Department, mounted on an ex W.D. chassis. The Etnyre, imported for runway work, could spray a road width up to 24' 0" and because road traffic was sparse much of the County Dublin work was executed in one width, with gritting by hand.[11]

The next year the firm was again successful in Eire with a tender for surface dressing in County Meath. This time a Sentinel combination sprayer was sent out, together with a living van for the crew and a Fordson supply tanker. Whereas the previous year the plant had been shipped out as cargo to Dublin, craned into and out of the ship's hold, in 1948 the vehicles were sent on the drive-on vehicle ferry from Preston to Larne which was then newly established using converted tank landing craft. At the border crossing at Dundalk the whole outfit was impounded by customs for three weeks whilst proper clearance papers and a sufficient bond were arranged. The crew had three weeks holiday camped in the caravan on the lawn of the Garda barracks, entertained by the cheerful and hospitable policemen. Tar for these contracts came by sea from Lancashire Tar Distillers at Preston. It was possible to pump some direct from the ship into the supply tanker but the remainder had to go into land tanks. In 1952 - 54 inclusive the firm won three seasons of spraying in South Armagh, Northern Ireland, but Sentinels were used only in 1952.

In the late forties and early fifties certain trade price associations - not connected with road works - did great harm to price co-operation by requiring the submission of identical prices by member companies, often at rates so high that they could not be considered to be related to costs. Although not then illegal such collusion brought warning comments from Government which were ignored. These refusals to listen provoked the passage of the Restrictive Trade Practices Act of 1956 which within five years or so put an end to price agreements. However, by one of the curious compensations of events which life affords, the phased cessation of coal gas manufacture in favour of natural gas from the North Sea and elsewhere meant that the tar spraying activities of the London Gas Boards came to an end so that the volume of spraying work available to contractors underwent a progressive increase that helped to ease the pains of the passing of price co-operation. In fact Glossops suffered no set-backs in profit that could be attributed to the ending of price fixing and it is tempting to draw two conclusions from this - firstly that co-operation had protected a number of less effectual firms and secondly that a fully efficient organisation was able to hold its own in open competition.

The worthwhile and swelling volume of civil engineering work secured in the immediate post-war decade particularly by the Birmingham and Bridgend area offices owed a good deal to the work which came the firm's way as a result of the airfield reconditioning programme set in hand in 1951 as part of the reaction of the Western alliance to the confrontation that had developed with Russia. In 1946 during the early stages of this optimistic period the firm had further expanded its civil engineering operations by buying the Yorkshire Public Works Co. Ltd. which it continued to operate as a separate company. In 1947 Hartshead Quarry was hived off as a wholly owned daughter company, the limited volume of road surfacing work which it carried out being subsequently transferred in 1951 to the then booming Birmingham office. Like many such surges in demand the crest in public works contracting was followed by a trough and in the two years or so from 1951 to 1953 the general situation changed from a sellers' market to a buyers' market. As a result there was a spell of much more keenly contested tendering during which the margin for profit and overheads was progressively reduced. In itself this would have been sufficient to lower the group's profitability but the situation was compounded by two major contracts, one at the Bridgend office and the other in the Birmingham area, in which unforeseen physical problems converted an already low profit margin into an alarming deficit, and by Yorkshire Public Works also running into financial problems. To add yet further to the difficulties Hartshead Quarry turned in a very substantial loss. The workings and problems of Hartshead are dealt with in more detail in the next chapter but it is sufficient here to record that it was soaking up monies earned by other parts of the group.

Besides all these financial constraints there was a further problem within the Glossop hierarchy. Since his election to the seat of power Henry Stephenson, always the dominant personality within the group of governing directors, had increasingly treated the firm as an empire with himself as emperor but because he had contributed so much to the company's development and had displayed such powers of leadership in time of adversity none had taken serious exception to his increasingly autocratic behaviour. It was, however, over his son John (Jack) that the four old colleagues came perilously close to falling out. Jack was an amiable and laid-back character of sybaritic disposition with many capabilities but manifestly not possessed of the dynamism and steel in the soul that had made his father such a force. Nevertheless Henry Stephenson made no secret of the fact that he looked upon Jack as his natural successor, to which end he installed him as the manager of the Birmingham area office and of the Hartshead operation.

In August, 1955, matters came near to breaking point. The previous year, ending August, 1954, notwithstanding losses at Hartshead, Bridgend and Birmingham, the group had still produced a profit of £30 913. For 1954/55, however, the net profit came down to only £987, a result that led to a fairly pointed boardroom wrangle. As a result Frank Willsdon, the Bridgend director, already close to retiring age, felt he had had enough and resigned, to be succeeded as a director by Cecil Warner. Elston, the executive director at Exeter, was discontented for further reasons. Firstly he had become increasingly impatient at his consistently profitable branch having been treated as an off-shoot of the London office and secondly, he questioned the way of allocating to it a share of the London office overhead which was done as a ratio of the profits earned rather than on turnover.

Apart from his understandable though misplaced desire to pass his position on to his son Henry Stephenson was shrewd enough to recognise that he had allowed the situation to slip away from him and as a consequence of the boardroom upset he agreed to set in hand a programme of reform. As a first step he appointed Victor Jones, a rising star who had been on the board since 1952, to report to him upon how the downward trend in profits might be reversed. On Hartshead, however, he remained adamant, maintaining that with the ever increasing environmental pressure upon quarries the time would come when it would prove to be a valuable asset. In the long term he might have been right but time was not on his side. Consequently nothing was done about Hartshead and losses continued to mount until by 1958 the cumulative loss exceeded £35 000, nor was much done about the management structure at Birmingham. In other departments, however, the reforms initiated by Victor Jones had begun to show an improved rate of profit earning.

Early in 1958, after considerable intermittent discussion, the three former governing directors agreed that Rupert Walton, senior partner of the firm of Leeds accountants, John Gordon, Walton & Co., who were the company auditors, should conduct an independent enquiry into the general conduct of the firm and make a report to the chairman. As 1957 progressed Henry Stephenson, by then in his seventies, had suffered a marked deterioration in his health. During his illness Ralph Willsdon, as next in seniority on the board, took over the chair. It thus fell to him to receive Walton's report which was dated May 20, 1958. Almost as he did so Harry Stephenson died, thus ending a career which had begun fifty-one years before when he became William Glossop's first assistant. In consequence the board elected Ralph Willsdon to continue his occupancy of the chair on a permanent basis.

[1] Conversation with the author 16.11.77

[2] Minutes of board meeting 11.12.34

[3] Minutes of board meeting 17.2.31

[4] Minutes of board meeting 8.9.31

[5] Minutes of board meeting 6.11.32

[6] Minutes of board meeting 10.7.34

[7] Minutes of board meeting 8.9.31

[8] Minutes of board meeting 5.9.34

[9] Personal communication from William Holbrow (London divisional engineer) to the author 24.3.77

[10] Letter from A. Rideal to F.W. Elston 30.8.55 (Amisfield House)

[11] Personal communication from L. Birkett Esq. to the author 15.3.78

Fig.33. An American Etnyre sprayer on a lengthened ex-WD Guy four-wheeled drive army gun tractor.

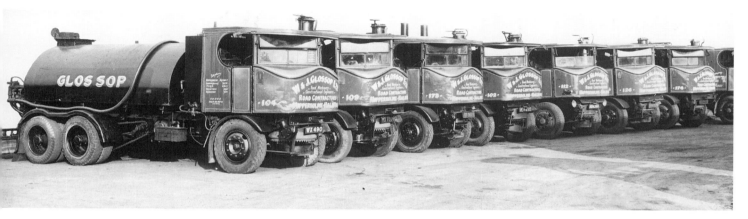

Fig.34. A line up of newly painted sprayers in the works yard at Hipperholme. All Sentinels, they are No.104 (7956), No.173 (8377), No.102 (8606), No.112 (8335), No.126 (5066), No.174 (8543), and No.162 (8284). The date is the early 1950s.

Fig.35. The first experimental road burner built on the Atkinson fleet No.126, withdrawn as a sprayer in 1939. Subsequent burners were combined with planers (see Fig.45)

Fig.36. By 1963 the Willsdon/Jones administration had brought about many changes in the plant fleet as is shown by this photograph of equipment, based on the York office, working near Wallsend-on-Tyne in June, 1963.

Fig.37. This photograph of an Ashurst sprayer on a Bedford TK chassis was taken at the St. Ives depot in 1967.

Chapter 5

The Concluding Years

Ralph Willsdon had succeeded to the chair by seniority rather than because he was by nature a reformer. On the other hand he recognised the good effects of the programme of changes that had been set in hand by his predecessor as a consequence of Victor Jones's investigations and, moreover, encouraged the latter into areas considered sacrosanct by Henry Stephenson. In particular this widening of the programme included discontinuing the use of steam driven vehicles and changes to the Birmingham area office and to Hartshead.

Rupert Walton's report in May, 1958,[1] had made it clear that he considered Hartshead Quarry had no commercial future, a point of view in which at least Arthur Rideal and F.W. Elston concurred[2] and with which Ralph Willsdon himself felt considerable sympathy. Nevertheless John Stephenson, who had inherited a large part of his father's shareholding, continued to point out that Hartshead Quarries Ltd. represented a very substantial capital investment which the board ought not to close without a final attempt to make it pay. In 1959, whilst this subject was still under fierce debate, John Stephenson lost his life in a road accident in Derby in which his car collided with a bus. Paradoxically this sad event which, on the face of it, removed a vigorous protagonist for the quarry and thereby made its closure easier, seems to have swayed the board in favour of keeping it open. Accordingly they appointed Charles Goodwin, an experienced Derbyshire quarryman, to manage the site. Goodwin made considerable improvements in the technical aspects of the operation but in the end the attempted financial rehabilitation was defeated by matters not under his control. The first of these was the geographical situation of the quarry within the Peak National Park which imposed expensive restrictions on both working methods and the siting of spoil heaps. The second was the distance of the quarry from the lucrative market presented by the road-stone deficiency area of London and the South East whilst the third was the geological problems of the site. These latter included moving large quantities of overlying sand, for which there was virtually no market, to expose the good hard white limestone. A further problem arose in that the good quality stone was banded with brown layers of inferior porous stone which was unsuitable for making tarmacadam because too great a proportion of the binder was absorbed into the aggregate. Any of these difficulties by itself might have been coped with. After all few quarrying operations are without some obstacles to their working but it was the conjunction of so many in relation to the one site that eventually forced the board to the unpalatable conclusion that the case for keeping Hartshead open was hopeless and working accordingly ceased finally in 1965.[3] The other area of the business in which John Stephenson's death had left a large enigma was the formerly profitable Birmingham branch which by the late fifties was losing money. A programme of retrenchment was instituted there with the ultimate purpose of closing the branch completely whilst minimising losses in the interim. The intention was to complete existing contracts, to undertake no new ones, and by progressive cuts to reduce the establishment to vanishing point. These cuts began at the apex of the pyramid with the then manager being replaced by his young second-in-command. To the surprise and delight of the board the ameliorating effects of this programme of reform were so rapid that a net loss of £4 000 in 1958 was turned round to a profit in 1959. In the face of this improvement the closure of the branch was first deferred and ultimately abandoned.

The anomalous position of the Exeter branch as an adjunct of the London area was abandoned making it an autonomous office under Elston, answerable direct to Head Office at Hipperholme. Though this made no difference to the shareholders it was a considerable morale booster to Elston whose branch was thus relieved of carrying an arbitrary allocation of London office overheads. In consequence of the reduced overhead it had to bear the Exeter branch became more profitable in the books so that Elston gained a well deserved rise in his own remuneration, an important element of which was made up of an annual bonus calculated upon the profits earned by the branch. Conversely the change meant that the whole of the overhead charge generated by the London office was thenceforth to be borne by the trade of that office so that London looked much less profitable in the accounts, a situation which Victor Jones set about improving by a series of economies that were finally completed a decade later.

The third change under the Willsdon/Jones regime was the move away from steam in the plant fleet and the eventual abandonment of the Glossop patent spray bar in favour of the Ashurst spray bar developed by Grant, Galloway & Gear Ltd. As far as is known Henry Stephenson had had no sentimental attachment to steam power but looked upon it as a well tried, reliable, and economical servant, the use and economics of which he understood and in the operation of which he considered Glossops to be well versed. In the early thirties the Road Fund Tax levels on steam vehicles were much increased when the Government adopted the taxation proposals set out in the

Salter Report. Consequently steam vehicles suffered a sharp decline in popularity in the hands of general commercial users so that sound steam chassis no more than ten years old - and many less - could be bought at derisory rates, a situation which became prevalent again in the forties and fifties during the terminal decline of road steamers. By contrast with general users steam road-making plant paid no Road Fund Tax. With considerable weight of evidence on his side, Stephenson was thus able to argue that since surface dressing plant was exempt from Road Fund Tax the pressures operating against steam in ordinary commercial use worked in its favour, in the case of firms such as Glossops, by depressing the cost of good second-hand units. For this reason he had continued to press the board to authorise the purchase and equipping of steam vehicles. However, as already noticed, as the fifties advanced it became progressively more difficult to recruit satisfactory drivers to manage steam plant and the Glossop made equipment. There was perhaps also a tendency to keep down capital expenditure by retaining old plant in service over long, a situation aggravated and explained, in some measure, by the post-1945 shortages of all types of new equipment. By the time of Stephenson's death in 1958 such dedication to steam had become virtually unique even amongst surface dressing contractors. In the forties Glossops had begun to use internal combustion engined chassis for sprayers in the case of smaller units, and under Willsdon's regime policy was reversed and the steamers were phased out in favour of motors. The last season in which steam played a significant part was that of 1965 and the last commercial work done by steam was in 1966.

During the last year of Stephenson's chairmanship the company had been offered, and had accepted, the opportunity to purchase Rowley Plant Ltd., a company in which he had had an interest. Based upon a depot at Beddington Lane, Mitcham, near Glossop's own yard there, Rowley was a company of medium size in its own field, earning a reasonable level of profit. Although there was nothing unusual about Rowley its assigned position within Glossops posed a question mark. On the one hand the board had decided that it had to remain independently managed and to stand, or fall, on its profit earning record. On the other hand they appeared to see it as a convenient source of plant, on which Glossop would have first call at what were obviously expected to be advantageous rates of charge. At the same time it was also thought that Rowley would be able to undertake repairs, again at advantageous rates, to Glossop's directly owned plant and, further, there was a certain amount of fantasizing about expanding the Rowley business on to a national scale without any corresponding committal to underwriting the level of capital outlay that would have been necessary. Rowley was thus required to pay its way, to have plant available to Glossops whenever it was wanted but at lower rates than its competitors, and to give the parent company's plant priority over other customers in the matter of repairs - clearly incompatibles. It fell to Willsdon's lot to sort out these irreconcilable aims. This he did by arranging for it to continue trading on its own merits, concentrating its work more or less upon its existing area of operations, receiving in return all suitable Glossop hire enquiries but no priority over other hirers as to acceptances. Any ideas of enlarging Rowley to take over the directly owned Glossop plant or to trade on a national scale were laid aside.

During the last four years of his tenancy of the chair Ralph Willsdon relied increasingly upon Victor Jones who had succeeded to the position of vice-chairman on Arthur Rideal's death in office in October, 1965. Consequently upon Willsdon's retirement on January 31, 1969, Jones was elected to fill the vacancy almost as a matter of course. Ralph Willsdon's departure finally severed the Glossop family links. Elston had already retired in 1963 and had been succeeded as the Exeter area director by Cyril Warner. Harry Peebles, a Scot who had joined the company a few weeks after William Glossop's death and had managed the York office for several years, was also made a director. For many years Arthur Rideal had doubled up his directorship with the post of company secretary though the duties of the latter post had been largely carried on by Ernest Milner who had been formally appointed secretary in February, 1953.

In the space of a year or two, therefore, control of the company stepped down, more or less, by a generation. The old regime had finally, and mostly involuntarily, relaxed its hold, and it is interesting to observe the direction which changes took under the new chairman and reconstituted board of directors. The reforms begun under Ralph Willsdon were carried on to completion. So far as organisation of the parent company was concerned staffing methods and duties were left largely untouched, and the changes which took place were mainly in routine transfers and promotion of staff, improvements in conditions of service, and a smoothing down of one or two rough edges inherited from the past.

Victor Jones had a more sharply defined vision than his predecessors of the course on which the company had to be set if it were to continue to prosper. As there was no longer a corps of governing directors, personally owning the bulk of the ordinary shares and thus able to ignore the possibility of uninvited take-over offers, any failure to produce an adequate profit return on the capital value would have made the firm vulnerable to hostile bids. He therefore found himself constrained to examine the way in which the undertaking was constituted and to determine which parts of it were truly assets. Having seen the Hartshead venture wound up at last he was now in a position to tackle other matters which he saw as a drain on the main business of the company. He also appreciated very clearly that it was no longer possible for the company to tread water in a decade becoming increasingly marked, as far as road making and repairing trades were concerned, by consolidation of ownership. It either had to go on or go under. In external matters, therefore, he set about increasing its share of the market whilst, at the same time, remaining clear of the conglomerates.

Examination of his aims as chairman must necessarily fall into two parts; firstly the changes made in the operation of subsidiaries and secondly the expansion of the company by absorption and amalgamation. The formation of 'groups', sometimes on an apparently haphazard basis, had been a fashionable feature of company administration in the latter fifties and early sixties. Despite the awful example of Hartshead Glossops unfortunately had not been immune to the malaise. As noted previously, the Yorkshire Public Works Company Ltd. was bought in 1946. Subsequently, again as already narrated, Rowley Plant was taken on followed by John's Motor Transport Company Ltd. (of Gorseinon, West Glamorgan) in 1958 and Sparkes Brothers Ltd. of Feltham, Middlesex, in 1962, small but reasonably successful companies engaged in roadworks and civil engineering. The next purchase was prompted by the recommendations of the Worboys Report on road signing, on which the present system of road signs is largely based and which was expected to lead, as proved to be the case, to a substantial increase in demand for signs. In anticipation of this in 1964 Glossops bought Allsigns Ltd. of Ascot, Berks, manufacturers, as the name implied, of all descriptions of road signs. Lastly, in the same year, the firm of D. Wendal Rosser Ltd. of Bridgend was bought - another road contracting firm.

Victor Jones was sceptical as to the overall value of these subsidiaries to the parent. Allsigns had been eclipsed by much larger competitors and was being priced out of the market; Yorkshire Public Works, whose management had somewhat overreached itself after a series of successes, had made a series of inexcusable losses; whilst John's Motor Transport and Wendal Rosser had lack-lustre performances. Consequently he decided that the subsidiaries were more hindrance than help. Wendal Rosser and Allsigns were wound down to non-trading status in 1970 and 1973 respectively but Yorkshire Public Works was disposed of by liquidation in 1968 and Sparkes Bros. Ltd. was sold to Bardon Hill Quarries Ltd. in February, 1969. The fact that Allsigns had not turned out to be particularly valuable to the parent company was, to some extent, merely bad luck as it had formed a logical adjunct to the other activities of the parent and complemented the road lining department of the main company which undertook road lining and lettering under the brand name *Glossline*. Owning small road contracting businesses engaged in the same classes of work as the parent had no such potential of usefulness.

In 1967 Glossops had been offered and had agreed to purchase the old established surface dressing firm of S. Sutcliffe & Son Ltd., based in Yorkshire. Sutcliffes was a family concern, turning over some 1.5 million square yards annually. The lesson had been learned and the new acquisition was integrated into the business, some of its activities being allocated to the York operation, then directed by Harry Peebles until he retired in 1976 and was succeeded by Eric Wass. Phillip Sutcliffe, the last active member of the old family proprietors, went to Glossops with his firm and managed surface dressing undertaken from the old Sutcliffe branch office at Spalding.

The company reached the mid-seventies with the subsidiary ventures largely cut off and the financial results at a satisfactory level. A major part of the programme initiated by Victor Jones when he had taken the chair was thus completed. The second phase, namely of reinforcing the base of the company without sacrificing its independence was a less tractable problem. The ideal solution might have been an amalgamation on equal terms with a similar company of roughly comparable status, preferably one which would have complemented the company's operations geographically. On the other hand the large road-stone groups had been self-evidently shopping for useful surface dressing contractors. Tarmac, for instance, had taken H.V. Smith & Company Ltd., another old established surface dressing firm, and the choice, therefore, was neither unlimited nor uncontested. Whilst these factors were under debate similar problems were being faced by another public company, Anglo American Asphalt Company Ltd. Based at Bishops Lydeard near Taunton, this company operated a quarry in the Mendips and another in the Quantocks and carried out contracting in the West Country, Midlands, and Scotland. At the end of 1971, with the appointment of Digby Burnell as Chief Executive, Anglo American Asphalt (AAA) had been given a necessary and vigorous administrative shake-up. Burnell, realising that AAA was too large to be dismissed as a minor operation yet too small to qualify for the major league, set about altering its situation. Having turned the company round from a loss making position to one of profitability he followed this up quickly by acquiring South Eastern Tar Distillers Ltd. in 1972. This group of companies included Johnson Brothers (Aylesford) Ltd., a long established surface dressing firm in Kent and South East of England.

In 1972 Digby Burnell wrote to Victor Jones suggesting they might meet. Quite unlike each other in either personality or temperament the two men soon found that casual conversational probing indicated an encouraging coincidence of views on the basic problems of their respective companies, the upshot of which was that a proposal was tentatively put together whereby Glossops would take over the surface dressing operation of AAA in return for shares and Digby Burnell would assume the chair of the combined concern on the retirement of Victor Jones. As matters were ultimately arrange he took over a year ahead of the latter's retirement and the two thus had a useful year in parallel with Burnell as chairman and Jones as president of the enlarged company. In 1977 a further rationalisation of operations was arranged between Glossops and AAA whereby Glossop took over an AAA subsidiary, the old established Somerset road contracting firm of W.J. King & Sons Ltd. (WJK), partly for cash and partly for shares, thus rounding off the Glossop spread in the Southern and Western counties.

Victor Jones's work as a reformer of technical and organisational methods was continued by the new chairman who initiated and carried through further changes in the internal structure of the company made necessary by the altered scope of its operations which had resulted from the amalgamation. Whereas it had never before had a strong connection in the South East - partly from the former predilection of Kent County Council for direct labour and partly because Johnson Brothers, as a local firm, had secured a large part of the available work - now it was very strong there. Moreover the former Johnson offices at Vale Road, Tonbridge, offered spacious accommodation well situated for the South East work. The London office in East Hill, Wandsworth, had been the apple of Harry Stephenson's eye. Stephenson had made London his base and had spent most of his time as chairman at the London office originally in Hammersmith Broadway. The post-war move to East Hill relocated the office in a pleasant eighteenth century house in its own grounds, far better than the Hammersmith offices, not far from his home at Barnes, which suited him well, but by the time 1976 arrived it had become an economic anachronism - difficult of approach by road; not well situated geographically in relation to the area managed from it; and encumbered with the heavy rates and outgoings arising from its situation in a London borough. Burnell, therefore, transferred the London supervisory functions to the offices, suitably altered for the purpose, at the London Area plant depot which by then was at Bell Farm, West Drayton, and created a Southern Region office in the office suite at Tonbridge from which the general administrative functions of the Southern Area could be carried on. Accordingly East Hill was closed and sold during the early summer of 1977.

In the same adjustment of administration a further regional office - Western Region - was based in Cumberland Road, Bristol broadly to administer the former AAA and WKJ interests, both firms having been very strong in that part of the country. This brought the number of regions to six; Northern, Southern, Midland, South Western, Wales, and Western. The old policy of treating each area as if it had been a separate operating company with head office as the holding company was not perpetuated. Each regional office was under the oversight of a board member but whereas in the days of the Stephenson administration board meetings had tended to consist of the 'governing directors' (Henry Stephenson, Frank Willsdon, Ralph Willsdon and Arthur Rideal) and one, or perhaps two, executive directors coming perhaps once or twice a year as spokesmen for or quite often defenders of their areas, the new board sat in full and its individual members relayed contract policy into the regions.

From the time that York tar distillery was amalgamated with Yorkshire Tar Distillers and therefore removed from their control, W. & J. Glossop had had their branded tars manufactured for them by arrangement with various regional distillers although branded tars played a progressively less important role in the trading of the company. Nevertheless limited quantities of trade-marked tar continued to be supplied until the phasing out, begun in the fifties, of coal gas production by the Gas Board removed a major source of tar, leaving coke ovens as the principal producers. As was noted in Chapter 3 sales of refinery bitumen, derived from petroleum distillation, were promoted with vigour in the inter-war years by the principal oil refiners and their subsidiaries and gained a substantial place - though less than that of coal tar - in the pre-war surface dressing market, either as straight bitumen or in blends of tar and bitumen. The diminished production of coal tar after the late fifties accelerated the movement of bitumen into the leading position so that after the uniting of Anglo American Asphalt interests with the basic Glossop business the group were very heavy buyers of refined bitumen, engaged in handling, storing, batching and, to some extent, blending on a considerable scale - in fact, such a scale as to lead to this section of the business being separated and expanded as Glossop Bitumens Ltd. from 1977. The company had manufacturing plants at Bristol and Exeter and storage depots at Caerphilly, Canterbury, Frome, Tonbridge, Cranmore, Bristol, and Shenstone.

With the closure of Hartshead participation in road-stone quarrying ceased for over two decades. However, for some years the company still operated the underground Law Hill Quarry at Southowram for the production of York stone flags and related items. This stone was used for pavings and copings in the Princess Hay Shopping

Centre at Exeter, a large post-war project opened by the Queen (then Princess Elizabeth) in 1949. Year by year, however, sheer economic pressure reduced the demand for natural York stone until the company decided in the early fifties to cease operations at Law Hill, removing the plant and capping off the shaft in 1965 against the day, regrettably unlikely, when a revived market might justify a reopening.

By reason of opposition on the part of Town Planning authorities, spurred on by the developing conservation lobby, the restrictions during the sixties and seventies on the opening of new quarries or extensions of old made secure aggregate sources of great strategic importance to processors and users of road materials so the lack of an independent aggregate source became a matter of concern to the Glossop directors. The amalgamation of AAA and WJK brought into the group the basalt quarries at Stoke St. Michael, Somerset, a source of crushed aggregate for road wearing course material, so that in 1978 the Glossop name was once again associated with the quarrying and marketing of stone as it was in the beginning.

After these changes the company had an annual turnover approaching £10 million, turning in a profit of a little under £750 000 before taxation, i.e. about 7.5% of turnover and around 29% on the capital employed. Hence despite the concern of Digby Burnell to protect it from predators, the company remained an attractive target, and with the emergence of the Thatcher Conservative government in 1979 these pressures progressively intensified.

During this period Shell had been making acquisitions in the black-top contracting industry through its wholly owned Colas group which had had its origins in the early twenties as Asphalt Cold-Mix Ltd., manufacturing cold bitumen emulsions. Begun by a Mr. Mackay it had considerable success. It was taken over by Shell in the late twenties and renamed Colas Products Ltd., going on to become the largest producer in its class. The reshaping of Colas in the 1970s into a road construction and surfacing group is far outside the scope of this book, but by the early 1980s it was seen to be shopping actively for useful businesses in this field. In 1983 it took over Dan Sullivan's company Allmacadams, and the next year this was followed by the acquisition of W. & J. Glossop Ltd. There was a short period during which the names of these two companies continued to be used but effectively the distinguishing characteristics of the Glossop firm as portrayed in these pages came to an end with the absorption into Colas.

[1] Report on file in Amisfield House

[2] Exchange of letters between Rideal and Elston, March/Dec. 1958 on file at Amisfield House

[3] File 'Hartshead' Amisfield House

A 1961 directors' meeting in the boardroom at Amisfield House. Those present, left to right, are Victor Jones, T.Stephenson, Arthur Rideal, Ralph Willsdon, Ernest Milner (the company secretary who was not a director), E.R. Brewster, F.W. Elston, and Harry Peebles. William Glossop's portrait is hanging above Ralph Willsdon.

Fig.38. *The Willsdon/Jones regime accelerated the withdrawal of steam units but the fresh plant could be almost as atmospheric as the old as this picture of Road Burner No.9 and its ex-military Scammell* Pioneer *demonstrates.*
[Road Roller Association Archive Collection]

Fig.39. *Tarspraying for the London Borough of Wandsworth, 1961.*

Fig.40. Glossops had a long-standing connection with Norfolk and in this photo from the early 1920's sprayer No.102 is seen at work on a rural road in that County.

Fig.41. Fourteen years or so later sprayer No.116 (Atkinson No.497 new in 1925 to Dewing & Kersley, the millers at nearby Fakenham) was photographed in June, 1938, at Docking, Norfolk, during its last season of work. On the right is the living wagon of the crew.
[Alan Duke]

Fig.42. During the latter part of the 1939/45 war a low-loader was built at Hipperholme, using the Sentinel DG4 No.8009, previously sprayer No.171 and before that owned by R.Rowley & Co. of Leicester.

Fig.43. Aveling & Porter 10 ton compound piston valved roller (No.9080 of 1919) bought by Glossops about 1933 from George Roberts of Caistor. It is seen here at Scunthorpe on Feb. 10, 1951, and was scrapped not long afterwards.
[photo by P.N.Williams. Road Roller Association Archive collection]

Fig.44. *The working gang posed with visiting notables at the laying of a stretch of Tarviated road at Balby for the West Riding County Council in 1907. Jimmy Glossop is to the right of the picture carrying what seems to be a book. The portly bearded man with the stick next to him is Jesse Ellis of Maidstone.*

Fig.45. *The success of former No.171 as the tractor unit of the wartime low-loader led to No.173 being rebuilt as the tractor unit of an articulated road-burning and planing set. Further such sets were built subsequently. In some the burners were under four separate banks of hoods as opposed to the single large hood seen here.*

Chapter 6

People and Places

Surface dressing always was, and remains, a strictly seasonal occupation taking place from Easter to October, but mostly from May to September so that from the beginning the bulk of the Glossop labour force was engaged only for about five or six months of the year. Nevertheless the chance of a few months of steady work was very attractive to the considerable number of men in the woollen and mining districts of West Yorkshire who, in the years before the 1914 war, contrived to make a living from casual employment. In many cases the same men came back year after year though there were a few for whom a single season was enough. The rapid expansion of Glossop's area of operation soon took them many miles from their homes in Hipperholme and Halifax. On these more distant contracts some lived in lodgings, others in tents or tarpaulin shelters which, in country areas, they put up by the road-side. As they were paid on piece rates they would work from sunrise to sunset on fine dry days to compensate for loss of earnings when the weather was wet and for this reason it was convenient to live together in a group. Moreover, as with steam engine drivers and coal heavers, the dirt associated with the job made them far from ideal lodgers and they were rarely able to get into good lodgings. Whilst it is true that many of the intended lodgers led rough lives at home there were times when even they drew the line at the grade of lodgings available to them.

Few names other than those of gangers have come down to us from the early days. The earliest list of gangers to survive is that for the 1911[1] season when there were five - Hardy, Crabtree, Beasley, Walker, and Kelly. Of these only Walker recurred in 1912 when seven were employed - Walker, Ames, Brannan, Perkins, Sykes, Dandridge, and Bell - and of these only Walker and Dandridge carried forward in 1913 when the number of gangers rose to eight. The new men were Somers, Leaning, Hullak, Holliday, Fouracre, and Faulkner. Wages varied between twenty-five shillings and thirty-five shillings a week. The earnings of the men who worked under these gangers were of the order of a pound to twenty-two shillings a week, according to output.

William Glossop's nephews, Ralph and Frank Willsdon, loved to recall those very early days and, in particular, their uncle's tight fistedness in dealing with wages and expenses. In view of the terrible struggles he had been through to keep himself solvent, when only a hairs-breadth stood between him and ruin, his unwillingness to spend a penny more than necessary was understandable. In one of the desperate moments he wrote to a creditor concerning a writ, 'Break me and you will get nothing, be patient and you will get everything'.[2] Even against this background his running battle with his gangers over 'slakings' is amusing, however. Road making in the summer being hot, dusty work it was maintained by the men that custom in the district required their employer to provide them with some free beer. William Glossop invariably demurred at the expense and on one occasion suggested oatmeal water as an effective substitute for beer, drawing the retort 'Nay, what's use of a sup if it deeon't mak' you feel no different'.[3] One supervisor entered expenditure on beer on his expense docket under the cryptic description 'EMB' which, on its being quickly and automatically questioned, he explained as meaning 'extras mainly beer'.

In the period between the wars as the staple industries of the West Riding - wool, coal, stone, engineering, and chemicals - were increasingly beset by shrinking demand William Glossop found no lack of willing takers for the summer work he had to offer. As the firm's operational area spread out ever further afield and the use of sprayers on steam wagons increased it became increasingly the custom to send out only the nucleus of each gang with the plant and to recruit other men locally, some of whom came back year after year. In this way the firm came to employ a good many men from Scotland and also from Norfolk. At the end of the spraying season many of the Norfolk men went on to sugar beet harvesting.[4] Many men continued to sleep in tents or bivouacs either to avoid unsatisfactory lodgings or simply to save money. The practice of sleeping rough in this way caused the younger directors some concern, and before the 1927 season they carried a resolution that, as a matter of principle, each tar-spraying wagon should be sent out with a living van for its crew.[5] Some of these living vans were made at Hipperholme but most were bought.

At this time a number of the leading men had become settled members of staff, winter and summer. Among them may be mentioned Jim Fouracre, who had been with the firm in pre-war days; Walter Jones, who had been one of the crew at the demonstration of the first steam sprayer in York in 1922; Frank Birkett, who drove it, later became a foreman, and finally went on to become depot manager at Hipperholme; and George Tasker, who in 1948 took charge of the depot set up at St. Ives, Huntingdon. During the winter they worked on plant maintenance and one winter Frank Birkett built a caravan for use with his sprayer, using the body of a Luton van for the superstructure and equipping it in accordance with his own ideas. His son Leon, later to succeed him as the manager at Hipperholme depot, recalls that when he and his brother were old enough they spent several summers with their parents in this caravan. Later Frank bought a large motor cycle and side-car. When on the move the caravan was towed by the sprayer and the combination was hooked on behind that with Mrs. Birkett sitting on the saddle to steer it. On right hand bends his father kept an eye on it to see that all was well whilst on left hand bends it was the mate's job to do so. On one occasion the tow parted on a hump-backed bridge whilst the mate was day-dreaming and the procession had gone on several miles before it was noticed that the final unit was missing! In one summer the sprayer and the Birkett family ranged from London to Perthshire and there is no knowing, now, how many schools the boys attended in those few months.

Living vans went on being used regularly with sprayers until the fifties. In the end two circumstances combined to reduce their use. In the first place certain licensing authorities began to question whether or not a sprayer licensed gratis as a road-making machine was entitled to draw a living van without infringing the conditions of the licence. Rather than run the risk of having to pay full Road Fund Tax on their sprayers Glossops and other spraying firms quietly dropped the haulage of vans behind sprayers. This meant the trouble and expense of arranging to move the vans separately. In the·second place the attitude of public health authorities towards van living had become increasingly critical, particularly in relation to sanitation or the absence of it. These two factors led to a decline in the use of living vans, though they did not disappear totally. With the reduction in numbers the older and less satisfactory examples were got rid of and a new stock of ex-R.A.F. vans was put into service. As these, in their turn, came up for renewal in the late seventies, their superstructures were replaced by residential type caravan bodies.

Each spraying gang was under the control of its own foreman or ganger, who sometimes doubled up as the driver of the wagon. In some ways there were good arguments in favour of the latter arrangement, particularly with a combination sprayer on which the gritter was attached to the wagon and both tar and grit could be controlled from the cab. The speed of the wagon and the height of the jets above the road were the two principal considerations in obtaining an even coverage without waste. Glossops had patented their own device (Patent No.210990 of 1924) for keeping the height of jets constant and fitted a low speed speedometer registering in yards per hour instead of miles to assist with accurate speed regulation, but the actual control rested with the driver. It was very important too that no escapes of water were allowed to come into contact with the road, whether from the cylinder drain cocks, the injector, or the ashpan. All these things were in the driver's province. Many drivers, such as Frank Birkett, doubling as foremen produced good work consistently. On the other hand a foreman, when driving the wagon, could not see what was going on behind him and if some small thing went wrong he would have gone some distance before it was noticed. A blocked jet might produce a band in the road neatly gritted but untarred, which circumstance could be very tiresome and time consuming to put right. Consequently as time went on it became increasingly the practice to keep the man in charge out of the driving seat so that not only could he watch the spray bar and gritter closely but also keep an eye on the sweepers and the roller driver. Drivers were required to be men of high stamina as Leon Birkett recalled in the following anecdote:

I joined Glossops in the Summer of 1945 and my first job was second man on an Atkinson steamer being delivered to Kings Lynn in Norfolk. The first day got us to Bawtry, the second day to Fosdyke in Lincolnshire where we slept on the waggon because we were so black nobody would take us in. The third day we reached Kings Lynn. We had to take on coal in Lincoln. The driver who was thirty years my senior (he lived to be ninety) carried the hundredweight sacks up a ladder to put them on top of the tank. .... When steam sprayers were phased out most of the drivers at Hipperholme became Heater/Planer foremen. They didn't seem to have the desire to drive petrol or diesel engined sprayers.

Because a steam sprayer might not return to the depot during the whole of the spraying season it fell to the lot of the driver and mate to keep it going during that time, carrying out minor repairs and adjustments, besides washing out the boiler weekly, oiling up, lighting up and clinkering off daily. In addition to these matters there was the continual need to keep an eye open for likely sources of water and the task of keeping the bunkers coaled up by the method described above. If a Sentinel boiler developed water tube trouble whilst distant from the depot the driver and his mate were expected to find a suitable grass verge, dig a hole in it large enough to take the firebox of the boiler, draw the fire and move the wagon in to position over the hole. When pressure was somewhat reduced they would blow down the remaining contents of the boiler or, if time permitted, allow it to become cold and drain it off. Meanwhile a set of sheer legs and a reconditioned firebox would have been sent from the depot. After the sheer legs had been rigged over the boiler, the flange nuts joining the two halves of the boiler together would be removed and the inner part of the boiler lowered into the hole by means of a block and tackle hung on the sheer legs. From there it had to be manhandled out of the way and the replacement had to be hoisted up and jointed in its place. Fortunately vandalism was rare in those days so that tools or parts of the dismantled boiler did not disappear mysteriously and wagons and living vans were seldom interfered with.

It was not only steam drivers who had to be resourceful. When Leon Birkett was driving the firm's first motor mounted sprayer in Ireland in 1947 the crown wheel and pinion broke up. He removed the broken parts but as it was a War Department four-wheeled drive chassis no spares were available in Ireland and they had to come from England. Pending their arrival he carried on working with it using the drive on the front axle which made steering rather difficult but kept the job going.

Spraying gangs were under the general control of outdoor supervisors or contract managers who were equipped with motor cycles for mobility. In the twenty formative years between the wars the directors and virtually everyone else in the management of the firm except William Glossop himself and the clerks in the head office took a share of this work. Perhaps the longest serving member of the outdoor staff was Vernon Walton who joined the firm in 1915 and continued for some forty-five years, during several of which he manned a tiny branch office at Grantham - one room and a telephone - from where he supervised the work of the firm in Norfolk and Lincolnshire. Another small office was set up at 71 George Street, Edinburgh, in March, 1930. Like Grantham, this was not an extravagant establishment - the rent was £28 a year.[6] In July, 1930, because of the volume of work in East Anglia and its scattered nature the firm appointed an assistant supervisor for the area, Arnold Kilner, at an annual salary of £350, a useful income for a young man in the Eastern counties at that time. Though the hours were very long in the high season many of them were taken up in the not uncongenial pursuit of riding through beautiful countryside on a motor cycle. A year later Mr. Kilner had the misfortune to be charged with fraudulent conversion of £29.8s.0d. arising from the sale of property of Melford R.D.C. Sudbury (Suffolk) magistrates committed him for trial at the Suffolk Assizes in July, 1931, pending which he was released on bail, during which period the firm felt obliged to suspend him from duty. The result of the trial being an acquittal he was reinstated with honour.[7] A happening like this was unique as far as the firm was concerned. A few pints too many on a Saturday night, the occasional fight, and motor offences from time to time were the limits of the usual run of charges and it was a relief all round when Kilner was found not guilty.

In some respects the company was a tough employer - grudging about holidays, expecting long hours, up to seventy a week, to be worked in the season without overtime and looking for total dedication to the job. There was also, particularly in Luke Bradley's time as secretary, a tendency to carp over trivialities. He is said to have grumbled that a messenger took a bus in Leeds when the tram would have been a penny cheaper. On the other hand an employee in real trouble, as Kilner had been, provided it was not of his own making, often found unexpected support and, as is revealed in various minutes of board meetings, members of staff ill for long periods were paid ex-gratia allowances for many weeks at a stretch.

The company wwas relatively early in the field compared with others in the industry when a staff pension scheme was introduced in 1951. Like many similar innovations it produced its own crop of malcontents. At that time Glossops tended to be a firm of old men, and those who had joined during the big expansion between the wars, particularly in the twenties, found themselves facing retirement on nothing more than the state pension. To ease their position the company contributed substantial initial sums into the fund. Thus a manual worker at Exeter, who shall be nameless, paid in a total of only £22.15s.0d in return for which he received an annual pension of £40.15s.0d guaranteed for five years - whether he lived or died - with the pension continuing for his lifetime. Thus for an outlay £22.15s.0d. he received a certain £203.15s.0d. and the possibility of considerably more.[8] Unfortunately in this case, as in most others, virtue had to be its own reward. Far from eliciting any appreciation the company's action in arranging this pension produced merely a surly growl about its meagre value compared with what younger men might expect to receive at the end of their service many years later and after years of contribution. For their part younger members often resented the older man getting, as they saw it, something for nothing. In this they were, perhaps, guilty of overlooking what some of the older men had put into the business. Soon after Harry Stephenson's death in 1958, F.W. Elston was able to write that in nearly thirty years service he had never had as much as half an hour off for illness and that the weeks holiday on which he proposed to take his wife the following month was the first time they had had away together for seven years.[9]

The intangible matrix which held the management of the firm together so closely was illustrated by another paragraph of the same letter in which he referred to his relationship with Henry Stephenson, the recently deceased chairman:

I can also look back, after nearly thirty years, with no regrets and, like you, we disagreed many times on policy but .... retained the privilege of private friendship ....to the end. I shall never forget how I joined the firm in the General Waiting Room of St.David's Station, Exeter, with a chat and a handshake and no agreement, beyond a gentleman's, and no promise or demand for an office.

Undoubtedly these words were written in a sentimental moment and the fraternal feeling was probably never quite as total as Elston was suggesting but it was a powerful - although probably not unique - ingredient in the success of the company. It co-existed, however, with the strange ambivalence of a work force made up, on the one hand, of employees of long-standing who in many cases had never worked for any other company and, on the other, of a large casual labour force engaged for some four months every year. It was these seasonal hands who provided much of the rich variety of characters and were the subject of the diverting anecdotes. Leon Birkett, for instance, recalled trouble during the contract in County Dublin in 1947:

> We had a large gang for hand chipping. They were local country men. One morning as we were about to start, the men went into a huddle further up the road. A sweeper, an ex-Connaught Ranger from the first world war, told the foreman, Arnold Dyson, the men were debating whether to strike then or wait until a length of road was sprayed. The foreman immediately ordered all the vehicles back to the depot at Swords about eight miles north of Dublin, leaving the gang to get back the best way they could. There were no buses. Not to be outdone, the foreman travelled to Dublin on his motorbike and recruited a new gang from one of the toughest areas in Dublin. Local men took one look at them and the strike was over. However, it was a case of out of the frying pan into the fire because the newcomers were certainly a rough bunch. Arnold Dyson had his hands full. He was a Halifax man, short in stature and as stubborn as a mule. He used to wear clogs and when he went into the Bank in Dublin to collect the money for the wages the crashing of his clog irons on the hard stone floor used to bring all activity in the Bank to a halt. He may have been the first man to introduce clogs into Ireland, who knows? The strikers wanted a halfpenny per hour more.

Such was the depressed state of employment in Eire during the 1940s that many of the men recruited as casuals had been unemployed for years and the foreman had to go easily with them at first until they became hardened up to work again. This and other circumstances of working in Ireland were something of a revelation to Glossop's men from West Yorkshire with its abundance of skills and manufacturing resources. Even coal, of which they had never known a shortage, was so scarce that they had to burn turf in the living van stove - not a highly satisfactory proceeding.

Another practice which they encountered in Ireland but which was seldom seen on their home territory was the droving of animals, cattle, sheep. and pigs, from place to place along the road. A stretch of quiet road might be tarred for the full width and the gritting in progress when a drove of animals would appear. Through either indifference or the inability to stop them the drovers would allow them to continue their progress across the wet tar causing some very peculiar contortions, though no instance was recorded of an animal falling.

On the whole, the drivers seem to have avoided disastrous accidents, though they had their share of lesser mishaps such as the one whose wagon skidded on a steep camber and came to rest without damage but with a telegraph pole between the cab and the body of the wagon. A potentially serious accident happened to Stan Appleyard when spraying on a steep hill in the Colne Valley. Although the wagon was in low gear he had omitted to secure the lever with the latch provided and, by mischance, it happened to slip out of gear on a very steep part of the incline with the result that the wagon began to run back. He shouted to his mate to jump off, which he did. The wagon ran backwards down the hill. Though the brakes could not stop it they checked the speed to the extent that the driver was able to keep it more or less on the road - itself no mean feat - until he reached a sharp turn. This he could not negotiate. The rear wheels hit the kerb and the wagon, already heavy at the rear from the gear mounted on it, reared up at the front and somersaulted into the gardens of some cottages several feet below. Miraculously no steam pipe or joint was fractured though the firing chute broke and hot coals were scattered in the cab from which the driver crawled unhurt. At the time - the early fifties - the engine had so little value that it was removed by cutting it up on the spot.

[1] Wages book preserved at York office

[2] Letter W. Glossop to James Clarkson (Letter No.237 - 9.10.10)

[3] *Glossops are Sixty*

[4] Communication to the author from Mr. L. Birkett 15.3.78

[5] Minutes of board meeting 11.3.27

[6] Minutes of board meeting 11.3.30

[7] Minutes of board meetings 31.3.31 and 3.11.31

[8] Letter A. Rideal to F.W. Elston 29.9.58, Amisfield House

[9] Letter Elston to Rideal 2.6.58, Amisfield House

Fig.46. *The late Will Riley photographed Clayton No.T1184 (sprayer No.162) at Blacko, Lancs. on July 11, 1934.*
[B.D.Stoyel collection]

Fig.47. (below left) *Although five Standard Sentinels were used by Glossops few photos survive. This is sprayer No.128 (Sentinel BS2230 of 1918), previously owned by John Smith's Brewery at Tadcaster.*

Fig.48. (below right) *The second sprayer No.171 (Sentinel 8385) on March 22, 1951, at Beddington Lane, Mitcham, with apron lettering shared by only a few other units in the fleet.*   [John H.Meredith]

59

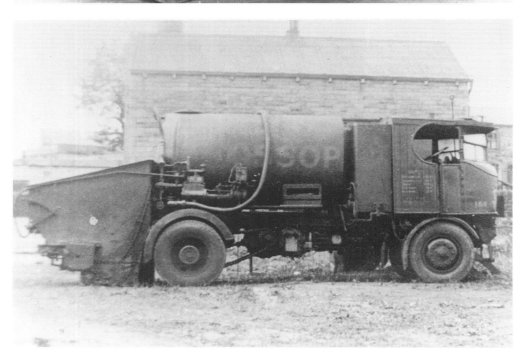

Fig.49. Sprayer No.169 (Sentinel 8681) was one of the last to run and was used well into the 1960s. Here it is in the yard at Beddington Lane in March, 1951.

[John H.Meredith]

Fig.50. The second sprayer to carry the number 125 was Sentinel 8730 (1932) built as a DG4 and rebuilt in 1944 by Glossops with a trailing axle and extended chassis to carry a 1500 gallon tank. Thus altered it served the Bridgend depot. It is seen here in the works yard before delivery to Bridgend.

Fig.51. Heavier road traffic and economic pressure had combined in the immediate pre-war years to make mechanical gritting increasingly attractive. Glossops bought a number of Bunce towed gritters for use behind steam sprayers before developing a gritter distributor for attachment to the sprayer itself. This meant a number of changes, including re-locating the tar pump on the offside of the tank. The gritter was driven by a roller chain from a sprocket on the offside rear hub. This is sprayer No.164 (Sentinel 7561) so fitted. It was scrapped in 1952.

Fig.52. Sprayer No.161, Clayton wagon No.T1150, taking on tar or bitumen from a railway tank wagon.

Fig.53. Sprayer No.137 (Sentinel 7506) began life as DG6 three-way tipper with the Forstal Ballast Pit at Aylesford, Kent, in 1928 and reached Glossops during the war. It was shortened to a four-wheeler, fitted with a 1000 gallon tank and equipped with a gritter box for use from the London depot.

Fig.54. Sprayer No.156 (Sentinel 8343) was a DG4 bought from the Cement Marketing Co. in 1938 and equipped with one of the older rectangular tanks for use in the London area. It ran until the end of the 1958 season.
[Roger West collection]

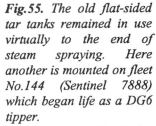

Fig.55. The old flat-sided tar tanks remained in use virtually to the end of steam spraying. Here another is mounted on fleet No.144 (Sentinel 7888) which began life as a DG6 tipper.

[Roger West collection]

Fig.56. No.157 (Sentinel 8311), bought by the firm after it was withdrawn by CMC in 1938, was another wagon that inherited one of the original flat-sided tanks. It is seen here at Beddington Lane in March, 1951, and ran until 1958.

[John H. Meredith]

Fig. 57. No.160 (Sentinel 7917) was the last Super to remain in use as a sprayer. In this picture it is at Beddington Lane in March, 1951, looking very down-at-heel but it worked in both 1951 and 1952.

[John H. Meredith]

Fig.58. The Worthington Simpson tar pump on sprayer No.169, one of the last steam sprayers to run. Glossops practically standardised on this make of pump.

[John H. Meredith]

Chapter 7

Particularly About Steam Engines

For the movement of stone from their quarrying interests Glossops relied mainly upon rail transport. Yew Tree Quarry was served by a 3'0" gauge tramway which involved a level crossing over St. Giles Road. The agreement for the construction of this was made with Hipperholme Urban District Council in 1919 and renewed in 1929. Both Penyghent Quarry and Glossops' new quarry at Horton-in-Ribblesdale were served by the Midland Railway, the Close Quarry at Embleton by the Cockermouth, Keswick & Penrith Railway which was worked by the London & North Western. At the Horton quarries there was also a system of narrow gauge lines bringing stone to the processing plant but, at the time of writing, no more sophisticated motive power than the horse and simple human effort is known to have been used.

On the other hand the partnership did use a fleet of private owners railway wagons based upon the Embleton Quarry and a photograph (Fig.11) exists of a line of these wagons. There were many private builders of railway wagons who were prepared to supply vehicles on a hire basis and straitened as he was on capital account in the first years of trading, William Glossop arranged for these wagons to be on hire. Mention of their hire occurs in some of the early balance sheets that were preserved at Amisfield House but no indication as to whom they were hired from. The only rail mounted equipment owned by the firm to appear in an inventory comes into that dated 1926, which included '14 Railway tank wagons £3444' and 'travelling crane £80'.

From the beginning of the surface dressing business until 1922 - a period of about fifteen years - the tar was either broomed in after heating in simple tar boilers or applied from horse-drawn hand pumped combined boilers and sprayers, such as the Bristowe *Cantar*. At the time of the 1926 inventory of plant there were forty-two hand pumped sprayers (valued at £80 each) and eighteen tar or bitumen boilers (at £50 each). There was also an asphalt mixer and a portable steam engine to power it. Later, particularly at Exeter, the pumped sprayers were mainly by Phoenix of Chard as opposed to the Bristowe *Cantars* used earlier and a number had paraffin or diesel engined pumps. Incidentally Exeter had no tanker sprayers until the early 1950s. Glossops seemed to have steered clear of the more exotic types such as the Coleman *Flapper*, on which the tar was applied through jets and beaten and spread by canvas flappers carried on a revolving drum, flail fashion, though latterly they did have one machine described in the stock book as an 'air pressure horse-drawn sprayer',[1] believed to have been of the Aitken type in which the piston of the air pump was driven by a crank shaft connected by a roller chain to the rear axle.

Haulage horses were hired from farmers or job-masters and any horses and carts required for grit distribution were similarly hired. Spreading of blinding grit was invariably done by hand shovel, sometimes from handcarts or horse-drawn carts but more often from small heaps strategically deposited at the road-side ahead of the spraying. The 1914-18 war, by its demand upon horses, made them both scarce and expensive, and by 1917 the firm was obliged to turn to steam haulage. Although wagons were almost as scarce as horses they managed to buy a 1908 Foden 5-ton overtype wagon (No.1720) from J. Graven & Sons, the engine dealers of Ely, Cambridgeshire. It is on record that the cost of overhauling No.1720 in March, 1917, and providing some new parts amounted to £436.6s.8d.[2], two thirds of the price of a new wagon. In the latter part of the year, two Clayton & Shuttleworth 5-ton overtypes (Nos.47987 and 48022) were bought direct from the maker's works at Lincoln. On the whole the Clayton & Shuttleworth was not a highly esteemed wagon but these two seem to have satisfied their owners as the first lasted until 1933 and the second until 1937. The firm thought well enough of them to add a third example (No.47349 of 1915), second-hand from York Corporation and this went on until early 1939. Two later type Claytons, T 1149 and T 1150 dating from 1927, built by Clayton Wagons Ltd. after the demise of the parent company, were not so successful and were sold. Two further second-hand Fodens were bought when the 1914/18 war was over. The first of these was 5-tonner No.4084, followed by No.4074, both of 1913. Later two Foden wagons were bought to carry sprayers and will be described shortly, but it was not until 1938 that more Fodens were added to the transport fleet. These were 5-ton tippers Nos. 7066 (1917), 11170 and 12090 (both of 1925) together with 6-ton tipper No.12798 (1927), but they lasted no more than two seasons.

These platform or tipper lorries were used for carting quarried stone, grit, tar in barrels or plant and equipment and were not directly involved in the spraying process. The use of steam wagons as self-propelling spraying machines began in 1922, as narrated in Chapter 3, more or less concurrently with the setting up of the partnership when the firm launched its campaign to secure a large share of the expanding market in surface dressing work. The economies found to be achievable with the *Autar* machines and the enhanced speed of execution made a decisive contribution to the success of Henry Stephenson's tendering. The sprayer which they evolved to mount on a steam wagon was of their own design, probably based upon their experience with the Aitken in which a cylindrical air receiver, pressurised by the air pump, was placed across the back of the vehicle, most of which was taken up by a rectangular tar tank. When pressure in the receiver had reached the desired level (which depended upon the viscosity of the tar being applied) the pump suction pipe was diverted from air to hot tar. In early examples this was done simply by dropping the filter end of the suction hose into the tar tank but later the more sophisticated arrangement of a three-way cock was adopted. The pump then continued to pump tar into the receiver until the working pressure was reached whereupon the delivery cock was opened, and tar descended to the spray bar and issued from four orifices with nozzles in the bottom of the bar. Thus the tar hit the road in a more or less solid jet which, it was hoped, would be spread out by the force of impact to cover the whole width beneath the spray bar.

By contrast, in the Glossop design of sprayer the pressurised tar was applied through two or more heads each containing nozzles which ejected the tar as opposed tangential jets so that as each pair of opposing jets met the tar was dispersed into a nebulous spray of droplets which reached the road surface as an even coating. Provided the tar was at the right temperature the machine was capable of doing a very good job, particularly with the relatively low viscosity tars of the twenties. A blocked nozzle, however, upset the system. With more viscous tars and, later, with the post-1945 trend more and more toward tar bitumen mixes or blends of bitumens it became less easy to work and the temperatures became progressively more critical. In this respect the sprayers on motor chassis, which were equipped with heaters burning kerosene or gas oil were able to cope better than the steamers which relied on steam heat to keep the bitumen fully fluid. When high viscosity bitumens were being sprayed the steam coils could not fully keep up with loss of heat in the contents of the tank. Therefore if the load was not applied rapidly there was a risk of what Leon Birkett once described as 'black spaghetti' being put on to the road instead of a nebulous spray. Spraying straight bitumens always imposed more work on the steam pump and whenever it could be heard to be working really hard it was a sure sign that the temperature within the tank had dropped.

The design of sprayer was patented as No.202,402 / 1923 in the name of William Glossop alone, but because of earlier patents with similar objectives the coverage of this patent was limited to details of arrangement and construction rather than any broad principles. The wording of the patent summed up what it covered in the following words:

1] A tar-spraying machine comprising in combination a steam-driven chassis carrying thereon a tar-tank having one or more steam-fed heating coils within it, and in addition thereto means to pass steam to said coil or coils from the steam-source provided for driving the chassis, a delivery-pump and pump connections for pumping tar from said tank to outlet-nozzles or for circulating the tar back to the tank, and in addition thereto a feed-water tank.

2] The subject-matter of Claim 1 combined with a filter within and co-axial with the steam-fed coil or coils, for the purpose described.

3] The subject-matter of Claim 2 combined with a coarse filter so disposed as to be in the path of tar supplied to the tank.

4] The subject-matter of Claim 1 wherein there is a charging man-hole for the tar tank with or without a coarse filter extending into the tar-tank beneath the man-hole mouth being shaped to cradle a barrel or cylinder thereon.

It was noted in the wording of the patent specification that:

considerable difficulty is frequently experienced by tar congealing in the feed pipes or spraying nozzles. In order to obviate this difficulty a pipe-connection 36 is provided between the pump and the boiler furnace of the steam wagon whereby hot flue gases can be drawn through the pump and passed through the conduits, nozzles, and control valves through which tar is passed in use. This will usually be done at the end of the tar-spraying operations before the tar has had time to congeal in the conduits and other parts.

The drawing does not make it at all clear how this was to be arranged and so far as can be ascertained it was not incorporated into the sprayers built under the patent. So far as is known - and I rely heavily upon Leon Birkett for this - such purging was always done with live steam. He was in a good position to know, his father having driven the first of the wagon mounted sprayers and for many years subsequently having been in charge of the Hipperholme workshop in which position Leon himself succeeded him.

The firm to whom Glossops turned to build their first sprayer was Atkinson & Co. of Preston, Lancs. Edward Atkinson, an established repairer of both fixed and self-propelling steam engines, had taken up the maintenance of steam wagons, particularly Sentinels, in the period before 1914 as they gathered commercial importance. When the 1914-18 war rendered new Sentinels practically unobtainable he had turned to making an undertype wagon of a design evolved in his own office. The new design of wagon based upon his own ideas and those of his chief draughtsman, J. Haythorn, whom he had recruited from Sentinel, was far more original than might have been expected in the context of the time and circumstances. It could perhaps be said that in its general characteristics it reflected the sturdiness and reliability of the Standard Sentinel but with remarkably few features that could be described as actually borrowed from it. Between 1918 and about 1924 these wagons enjoyed a modest popularity which declined in the mid-twenties, on the one hand because of failure to keep the design up to date and, on the other, because of financial and personal problems within the firm. It is not known how the firm was introduced to Glossops but it was a fortunate choice - big enough to carry out the scheme satisfactorily yet small enough to be interested in a project yielding a total income of a little over a thousand pounds.

The first wagon carried the Atkinson works number 306 and was delivered in May, 1922. Tar was carried in a flat topped 1000 gallon tank with provision for steam heating by internal coils and the spraying operation was controlled from a platform at the rear. The new sprayer had such an outstandingly successful season in 1922 that in March the following year it was joined by No.388 and by four more (Nos.423, 441, 442, and 443) in the next year. The contract price for the first Atkinson sprayer in March, 1922, was £1150, the second, a year later, cost £1095, whilst the third (January, 1924) came to £1230.[3] In the same document the value of the two Fodens and two Claytons was put at £1315. By the time of the inventory of 1926 the Atkinson sprayers numbered 101 to 106 inclusive were valued at a total of £7050. Atkinson No.423 (Fleet No.103) was shown on Glossops' stand at the 1927 Public Works Exhibition. That year Harry Stephenson had secured the contract for surface dressing Piccadilly, London - a considerable feather in his and the firm's cap - and the work was carried out with Atkinson machine sprayers, a point made much of in the advertising on the stand. As will be seen from the illustrations of these first wagon mounted sprayers there is evidence of experiments in the layout of the pumps and ancillaries but neither written or oral evidence survives as to the form these took so that the photographs remain the sole record.

On the other hand the changes made in sprayers 104 and 105 (Atkinsons Nos.441 and 442) represented more than minor adjustments. Atkinsons had been experimenting with a towed sprayer for bitumen in which the tank was heated directly by a coal fire and the contents were forced from the jets at a pressure between 60 and 80 psi by heated compressed air by Atkinson's patented combining nozzles. The pressurising was intended to be done by a steam driven air compressor taking steam through a flexible pipe from the steam tractor towing the outfit. In Glossops' Nos.104 and 105 this arrangement was adhered to with only minor alteration. The wagon chassis was made longer and the tank was placed at the extreme rear leaving space between the bitumen tank and the water tank for a Westinghouse compressor. So far as one can judge the wagons were not successful and were changed to tar sprayers using Glossops' own spray nozzles minus the Westinghouse pumps before delivery to Glossops.

In all Glossops had at least thirty-three Atkinson wagons (out of a total Atkinson steam production of about 325), but a number of these were bought second-hand. The last wagons bought entirely new from Atkinsons were Nos.529 and 530, acquired in 1928 and 1930 respectively when the original Atkinson business was teetering into ruin. The first sprayer had a working life of ten years but was not actually scrapped until 1934, out-living by a year the second which was broken up in 1933 although it had not worked after the end of the 1930 season. The Glossop sprayer fleet was numbered in a series beginning with 101. Curiously enough the wagon which took the number 102 after Atkinson No.385, the first bearer of it, was withdrawn was an older Atkinson, No.168 of 1920, which had been new to Associated Portland Cement Manufacturers Ltd. and came to Glossops in December, 1930, from Sentinel Waggon Works (1920) Ltd. at Shrewsbury where it had been taken in part exchange for a new wagon. Sentinel were the source of several of the second-hand Atkinsons purchased by Glossops about 1929 and 1930. In the autumn of 1929 the price of an Atkinson tanker and trailer was about £250! As the Atkinsons had only a single road speed against the two speeds offered by most of their competitors, except to one or two faithful users they were out of step with the requirements of 1930 and consequently cheap second-hand.

The Glossop Atkinsons were on solid tyres and, on the whole, were not deemed worth the expense of converting to pneumatics. Their only Atkinsons to be converted were No.496 of 1925, which replaced the original fleet No.112 in 1933 and continued in use until the end of the 1939-45 war, No.126 (of which the works number is not recorded), and No.127 (Atkinson 458). Changes in the Construction & Use Regulations mooted in 1939 would have made it virtually impossible to continue the use of solid tyred sprayers. Because of the outbreak of war this was not put into effect but by that time the firm had arranged the replacement of almost all the remaining Atkinsons still on solids. The last solid tyred Atkinson sprayer (works No.519) was given a reprieve by the war and ran until 1942. After the war when a chassis was needed for use under the first Glossop road-heating machine No.126 (GB7038) was selected. The position of this wagon in the Glossop fleet list was anomalous in that a replacement for it, Sentinel Super No.5066 of 1923, had been bought and allocated its number in 1939 but the Atkinson had remained intact at Hipperholme, possibly as a strategic reserve against loss of more recently acquired wagons.

The replacements for the Atkinsons were second-hand Sentinel undertypes, bought at intervals through the second half on the 1930s. Some of the units purchased were the single speed Super but the preponderance were of the two speed DG type. Preference was given to wagons either built on or already converted to pneumatic tyres. Latterly six wheelers were the most sought after as the extra length enabled an 1,800 gallon tank to be fitted, thereby extending the range on one tank filling. Whilst it would be tedious to attempt to discuss all the Sentinels in detail the career of one or two units may be traced. Super Sentinel No.6400, which carried the Glossop fleet number 120, was built in 1926 and used by Topham Bros. (Manchester) Ltd. until 1937 when Glossops bought it and converted it into a sprayer on pneumatic tyres. It spent nearly ten years in this function until, in the post-war period, it was decided to eliminate the few remaining single speed wagons from the sprayer fleet mostly because keeping them at a constant speed during spraying demanded a higher degree of attention from the driver. The wagon was, however, still in good running order and as there was a shortage of other suitable chassis it was decided to reuse it as the unit of articulated road burner No.RB3. In this form it went on for ten years more and was finally withdrawn in 1956. Another Sentinel wagon that had a similarly varied career was Glossops' No.117 which started life as a Sentinel DG six wheeler (Works No.7948) with Kinder Bros. of Blackburn in 1929 passing to Glossops in 1940 through the agency of Service Garage, Brighouse - through whom many Glossop vehicles were purchased - when for some reason it was cut down to a four wheeler and fitted with spraying gear. Like its sister wagon No.120 it was converted to the unit of a road burner just after the war and served in that form until 1952. Two other articulated road burners were built using cut-down Sentinel DG6s as the motive power units. The earliest of these was No.8099 bought in 1943 and previously used by James Brown & Sons of Aighton, Lancashire and the Sandywood Sand & Gravel Co. The other was No.8768 which did not join the Glossop fleet until 1946, the previous owner being the Goole Tillage Co. Both of these worked until the late 1950s.

Although the majority of the Sentinels operated by Glossop were either Supers or DGs they also had a small number of the earlier Standard Sentinels. One such was fleet No.125 (Sentinel Works No.AS3190), previously owned by the National Fuel Oil Co. and hence having the advantage of already being a tanker. Another Standard was fleet No.128 taken over in 1933 from John Smith's Tadcaster Brewery (Works No.BS2230). There were six further Standards, the fleet numbers of which are not recorded. In two instances, both tankers bought from the National Fuel Oil Co., the Sentinel works numbers (AS3211 and AS3482) are recorded, but in respect of the other four even this information is absent. Two of the four were used as sided lorries, the others as tankers, All the Standards were on solid tyres and had been scrapped by 1942.

After the end of the 1939-45 war the company bought seven shaft-drive S-type Sentinels from Annis & Co. of Hayes, Middlesex. Earlier still these had been owned by the Cement Marketing Co. Ltd.. These wagons, all dating from the winter of 1933/34, were light, fast and manoeuvrable but lacking the robustly unbreakable qualities of the earlier models. Of the seven, three (Nos.8872, 8873, and 8874) were four wheelers, and the remaining four (Nos.8878, 8879, 8880, and 8881) were six-wheeled. These wagons stood for some time at the Glossop depot in Beddington Lane, near Mitcham, Surrey, becoming steadily more derelict. and eventually all were broken up. Whether or not any were used in revenue earning service is questionable. The reasons for buying the S-type Sentinels are not clear after this lapse of time. It may have been that at first the intention was to introduce them to the sprayer fleet but this was overtaken by inertia or the realisation of how much effort would have been involved. A further S-type Sentinel said to have been owned by W. & J. Glossop came from R.M. Woolley of Bucknell, Salop, in 1960[4], but Leon Birkett believes it was bought by his father, Frank, personally with a view to preservation, which it failed to achieve. Although Foden wagons were popular with some of their competitors as the basis for sprayers as far as can be determined Glossops used only two for this purpose. No.12566 (1927) was bought from Illingworth, Wood & Co. Ltd. of Bradford and last used in 1944, and No.12830 (also 1927) which came to the firm from West Riding County Council in 1936 had a life of only three years.

Three other makes of steam wagon were used as sprayers. One Leyland (No.F2/120 - built in 1926) was bought in 1930 from Atkinson Walker Wagons Ltd. and scrapped in 1933, and two late type Claytons (Nos.T1148 and 1150 of 1927), bought about 1934, were last used in 1938. One other late type Clayton (No.T1149 of 1927) was a sided wagon and was last used in 1937. Three examples of the Yorkshire, the only other make of steam wagon represented in the fleet, were used, though not completely concurrently. Fleet No.122 (Works No.1401 of 1921) was already a tanker when it came from the Shell-Mex group in 1927 so that only spraying gear was needed, and the following year a further example (No.1386 also of 1921) was bought. A third Yorkshire (No.1169 of 1919), a straightforward sided wagon bought in 1931, seems never to have been licensed by Glossops. The whole cost of the Leyland sprayer, incidentally, was £230.[5]

As a matter of policy the company did not set out to own steam rollers preferring to hire from one of the national hirers. In the twenties and thirties a great deal of this hiring went to the Eddison Steam Rolling Co. Ltd., who had branch offices at Chestnut Street, Darlington, managed by Lionel James, and in Kingston, Surrey, managed by Roy Colley through whom much of the hiring was placed, though some went by way of the Dorchester head office. This policy weakened somewhat as the 1930s advanced, probably because it was found that steam rollers in working order were available very cheaply, making it more attractive to operate directly owned rollers. That longest in service was probably Wallis & Steevens *Simplicity* No.7832 of 1926, weighing only a nominal 3 tons and fitted with an inclined boiler, which was bought in 1933 from E. Parry of Putney, London - not far from Harry Stephenson's home - and sent to the newly set up branch at Exeter where it stayed until 1959. In the North of England the firm also used three rollers by Thomas Green & Co. Ltd. of Leeds, whose products were noted for their ability to cope with the hills of their native terrain. Of these the largest and oldest was No.1485 of 1905, nominally of 12½ tons weight, which was bought in 1938 from W. Thackray & Son of Old Malton, Yorks. The others were Nos.1659 (1911) and 1870 (1915) both of about 10 tons nominal weight. The second of these came in 1931 and was not scrapped until 1951. There were nine Aveling & Porters, the oldest of which was No.4341, built in 1899, and three Marshalls. Marshall No.82101, an S-type dating from 1927, came to the Glossop fleet in 1937 having spent its first ten years with Beddington & Wallington UDC with whom it had led a very leisurely existence. Apart from the *Simplicity* already mentioned there were three other Wallis & Steevens rollers. Of these No.7941, a 10-ton *Advance* built in 1927, was the last to remain in Glossop hands and survives in preservation. The company also owned sundry motor rollers, of which virtually no details survive. Probably the earliest was a Green's petrol engined roller which was already owned in 1926.

The steam stock was completed by two traction engines. The earliest of these was Wallis & Steevens 6NHP expansion engine No.7456 built in 1917 for the War Department and bought soon after the war for hauling and powering a portable tarmacadam mixer. The other was a more recent single cylinder engine, again of 6NHP, built in 1934 at Gainsborough, Lincolnshire, by Marshalls, which was bought from William Thackray & Son and used briefly to power an asphalt plant in the North East. This is now preserved.

It was not until the 1939-45 war that the company made extended use of motor lorries despite having made a tentative beginning with the internal combustion engine by the time of the inventory of 1924[6] when the rolling stock included two Thornycroft petrol engined lorries (valued at £830 for the pair), a Humber 11.4 car and a model T Ford. There were also four motor cycles ridden by the outdoor supervisory staff. By 1926 the two Thornycrofts had been joined by a Karrier, a Belsize, and a de Dion, and the motor cycles had gone up to seven, but the Ford had disappeared. In 1927[7] the board authorised Harry Stephenson to purchase a Fordson tractor for £272.5s.0d and two trailers (£494.5s.0d the pair) for use in the London area, probably for grit carting, but in the 1930s replacement petrol vehicles were mainly 3 ton Bedfords or Morris Commercials. During the war the number of petrol engined trucks in service went up, in part from authorised purchases of new vehicles, mainly the civilian version of the military Bedford 3-tonner, but also a number of second-hand chassis of whatever type happened to be available.

During the war the Ministry of Supply imported several American made *Etnyre* sprayers with motor driven pumps and oil fired heating, and after the war Glossops purchased some of these *Etnyres* second-hand from the Ministry and others new via Jack Olding Ltd., the UK agents. The first Etnyre was mounted on an ex-W.D. four wheeled drive Guy and sent to Ireland in 1947. Another was mounted on a second-hand Morris *Leader,* another on a Dennis, and others on Thornycroft *Tridents*. Despite the post war scarcity of new truck chassis or even good second-hand examples, during the late forties the fleet was augmented by 3 and 5 ton Bedfords in both short and long wheel-base versions, Austins, various American Dodges and Chevrolets, Thornycroft *Tridents*, Morris Commercials and ex-W.D. Guys. It must be remembered that steam wagons still formed the backbone of the fleet. Whereas a new Austin cost £680.16s.0d nett the price of a Sentinel steamer in full working order was only £110.[8]

When the first, and mainly experimental road heater was built up on the pneumatic tyred Atkinson steam wagon its function was limited to softening the old surface which then had to be removed with hand rakes and scrapers. The next development in the design, therefore, incorporated in addition horizontal scraper blades to remove the softened surface, with a conveyor to transport the planed-off material to a waiting tipper lorry being towed backwards behind the outfit on a chain. It was the length of chassis required to accommodate this machinery plus its fuel tanks and engine that dictated its arrangement as a semi-trailer coupled to a Sentinel unit. Six further burners were made up in this way before it was decided to go over to the Gardner engined Scammell *Pioneer* six wheeled military tractor for the motive power. The first of the Pioneers was bought in 1959 for less than £600 and twenty years later was still serving its purpose effectively and reliably. Subsequently other Pioneers were bought for use as depot recovery vehicles.

By the late fifties, partly because of Harry Stephenson's conservative policy on plant replacement and partly because of his belief in steam as a propulsive power, the firm's equipment had begun to acquire the rather less than helpful reputation of being slightly quaint. The commercial significance of this was slight for most of the contracting work was obtained by the straightforward expedient of submitting the lowest tender but it tended to have a demoralising effect on the younger and more ambitious members of the staff. Nor was it entirely untrue to say, as was, indeed, done in the exchange of letters between Elston and Rideal quoted in Chapter 3, that unreliable spraying plant was costing the firm money. The modernisation programme, instituted under Ralph Willsdon and largely implemented by Victor Jones, at first as Vice Chairman and later as Chairman, reversed the situation in less than a decade. Probably the most important decision was to adopt the Ashurst-Johnson sprayer as standard equipment for the group, which not only improved performance but also reduced plant maintenance costs. Because the mileages covered by surface-dressing vehicles, whether on spraying or gritting duties, are small their chassis have a greater life expectancy than in long distance road haulage but nevertheless by the seventies the Glossop fleet was modern. Products of the British Leyland group predominated in all classes of vehicle, but Bedford and Ford were well represented and there were also a number of units by Foden.

The improvement in spraying performance brought about by modern spray bars is not, perhaps, commonly realised. The techniques of measuring deviations in distribution of binders use apparatus largely developed by the research departments of the London Gas Companies and cannot be discussed in detail here but they record the deviation of actual from average distribution. Before 1956 a deviation of 20% or less was considered good and was the permitted deviation under Road Surface Dressing Association rules. In 1956 this was dropped to 15% to be followed by a drop to 12½% in 1968. Eighty-four per cent of the sprayers tested under the R.S.D.A. annual testing scheme showed 10% deviation or less. Gratifying though this result was it must be remembered that it came from a test conducted only once a year and that deviation between tests could increase unless the plant was watched carefully and given proper maintenance.

Traditionally the Glossop fleet colour was a deep maroon with black underworks, written in shaded and blocked letters in yellow or gold except in London where, in the latter days of steam, many sprayers were in all-over black. Anglo American used a deep green for many years and Johnson Brothers and Sutcliffes a mid-green, but before the amalgamation Anglo American had decided to adopt a yellow livery and black lettering, in line with the results of research on plant visibility sponsored by the Department of the Environment (as successor to the Ministry of Transport). At the amalgamation the decision was taken to standardise this for the group and to adopt a new logo and simplified sans-serif lettering. As a reminder of the past, however, and to preserve an example of the old type sprayer in its working livery, in 1977 the firm reconditioned the last steam sprayer in its ownership. This vehicle, Sentinel No.8666 built in 1932 and bought by Glossops in 1952, had been kept in store at the Hipperholme depot since the mid-sixties and it was decided to mark Jubilee year by recommissioning it for appearances at shows and veteran vehicle rallies. Subsequently this was transferred to the Tonbridge depot but was eventually sold into preservation.

[1] Assessment of assets 31.1.24 - Amisfield House

[2] Letter W.J. Glossop to Inland Revenue, Halifax 1.3.22

[3] Note in inventory file, 1924 - Amisfield House

[4] Journal of Road Locomotive Society - Vol.52 No.4

[5] Inventory of plant and assets, 1926 - Amisfield House

[6] Inventory of stock, 1924 - Amisfield House

[7] Minutes of board meeting 2.12.27

[8] Details of Capital Expenditure, year ending 31.1.49 - Amisfield House

Fig. 59. *The classic tarspraying scene of the 1950s. The Bedford OY sprayer was seen in Fig. 32 when new in 1942. Here after 15 years of service, latterly in the Exeter area, the gloss has been worn off.*

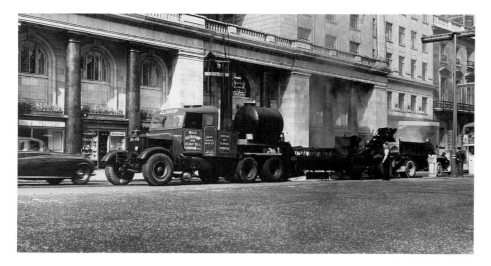

Fig.60. In 1959 Glossops bought the first of several ex-W.D. Scammell Pioneers for use with a heating and planing outfit. Here one such unit is working in Piccadilly, London.

Fig.61. Within the company there existed a dichotomy between those, like Rideal and Elston, who wished to see a sleeker and more modern image and the Stephenson faction who believed steam to be a trustworthy and reliable motive power. The modernising faction succeeded in having a number of motor sprayers given what was facetiously referred to as the 'limousine treatment'. JWU 929 was destined for the London depot but a second one (JWX 220) was made for Bridgend. One undesirable effect was the trapping of burner and exhaust fumes on the control platform, leading them to be dubbed man-killers. *Both vehicles had Etnyre sprayers.*

Fig.62. The phase of boxing everything in was short-lived and this sixties sprayer, also for Bridgend, demonstrates a more functional approach. The sprayer equipment here is by Ashurst.

Fig.63. Sprayer No.119 (Sentinel 8694), a wartime acquisition, posed outside Amisfield House with a Bedford OY supply tanker. The date is believed to be just after the end of the war.

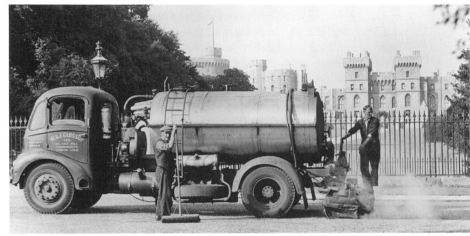

Fig.64. Glossops enjoyed depicting their plant against Royal backdrops. Here a sprayer on a Thornycroft Trident *is working in the vicinity of Windsor Castle.*

Fig.65. Road burner No.1 at Horsforth, Yorks. on May 2, 1954. The Sentinel works plate was 7945 and the registration RX 3147. Whether or not either represented its true identity is problematical (see Appendix).

[Brian Shaw]

Fig.66. Another identity riddle parked up at Hemsworth, Yorks. on April 23, 1957 - Road burner No.2 then carried Sentinel works plate 7296 and the registration GN 5753. (see Appendix).

[Brian Shaw]

APPENDIX - Glossop's Steam Vehicles

The following pages represent the best summation I am able to make of the 133 or so steam wagons and 22 other steam vehicles that passed through the firm's hands. The bulk of the research upon which this is based was that carried out by my friend, the late Alan Duke, supplemented by such information as I was able to retrieve from sources within the company and by details supplied by other friends and acquaintances. No enduring or comprehensive vehicle records were kept by the company. Moreover, because of rebuilding and the intermingling of the parts of various wagons, from time to time Glossop steam vehicles could be caught wearing a brother's clothes. To cite an instance, the Sentinel wagon registered as TE 9861 bore the works number 8099 but spent several of its latter years carrying the works plate of No.8768.

The sprayers, being classed as road-making machines, were not required to pay road tax. In the latter years of steam the large yard at Hipperholme works invariably contained a number of wagons which, in the terms of the theatrical profession, could fairly be described as 'resting'. Some never turned a wheel again and were merely kept to be robbed of parts. Others, when a surge of demand required it, went out to work again whilst, most reprehensibly, it is suspected that when a serious failure occurred in a wagon licensed for use it was easier to swap its number plate and makers plate on to a 'resting' wagon than to go through the time wasting charade of a gratis licence. This makes it difficult to say with certainty the last spraying season during which a particular wagon was used. Nor would it be much easier if one were to change the description to 'last year available for use' because again the problem of defining 'available' is ever present. If one is to be literal, a wagon whose mechanical lubricator had been 'borrowed' was not available but could have had the deficiency remedied almost within minutes had it been required urgently. In short the dates of finishing work are better looked upon as indicative rather than definitive, and the actual identities of some of the longest lasting wagons are in doubt. By the end of steam they had been so hybridised that it would be hazardous to attempt an absolute identification. Road burners Nos.1 and 2 form a convenient instance. In 1954 the tractor unit lettered RB1 had the registration RX 3147 and the Sentinel works plate 7948. This registration came with Sentinel 7561 (Sprayer No.164). The works No. 7948 belonged to Sprayer No.117 which had been registered as CB 9387. In 1957 the tractor lettered RB2 bore the registration GN 5753 (originally on Sentinel 8452) but had the Sentinel works plate 7296, probably off one of the wagons bought for spares but never (officially) used. Life is indeed a mystery!

Abbreviations
The following abbreviations have been used in the tables:

Makers

A	Atkinson	A&P	Aveling & Porter
C	Clayton Wagons	JF	John Fowler
CS	Clayton & Shuttleworth	TG	Thomas Green
F	Foden	ML	Marshalls
L	Leyland	W&S	Wallis & Steevens
Y	Yorkshire		

Types (applicable to Table 3)

CDO	Compound with overhead slides
S	Single cylinder
CDS	Compound with slide valves in side valve chests
CDP	Compound with piston valve

Column headings
Most are self explanatory but the following notes may help:

Finished: The date given is the last spraying season in which the vehicle is believed to have been used.

Type: This column states whether the wagon was on four or six wheels when bought. In the case of Sentinels, it is further amplified to whether a DG, Super, or 'S' type. In the case of Standard Sentinels (such as fleet No.128) the works number is preceded by the letters AS or BS, the first letter of each indicating whether the wagon was an 'A' or 'B' type Standard and the 'S' that it was equipped for hauling a trailer.

Remarks: This obviously includes miscellaneous information. The letters 'RB' stand for road burner.

Previous operator: This column is intended to indicate the last owner before Glossops to operate the wagon in commercial use. Thus dealers are excluded but in the case of the 'S' types bought in 1946 it is questionable whether or not Annis & Co. actually used them after purchase from CMC and before selling them on to Glossops.

TABLE 1 - STEAM SPRAYERS & TANKERS

Fleet No.	Regn.No.	Make	WorksNo	Year	Previous operator	Bought	Finished	Type	Remarks
101	WY 3567	A	306	1922	New	1922	1932	4	
102. [1]	WY 7589	A	388	1923	New	1923	1931	4	
102. [2]	CK 3201	A	168	1920	Cement Marketing Co.	1930	1938	4	
102. [3]	VE 6492	S	8606	1931	Hovis Ltd.	1952	1965	DG4	Pneumatics
103	WT 3134	A	423	1924	New	1924	1934	4	
104. [1]	WT 4234	A	441	1924	New	1924	1935	4	
104. [2]	WX 490	S	7956	1929	J.Smith, Tadcaster Brewery	1936	1953	DG6	Pneumatics
105	WT 4685	A	442	1924	New	1924	1939	4	
106. [1]	WT 4686	A	443	1924	New	1924	1942	4	
106. [2]	OD 1572	S	8666	1932	Wilson & Kyle, Brentford	1943	1965	DG6/4 T	Pneumatics: carried works plate 6400
107	GB 7165	A	468	1924	New	1924	1935	4	
108	GB 7582	A	473	1925	New	1925	1938	4	
109. [1]	WW 6206	A	529	1928	New	1928	1943	4	Converted to pneumatics 1937
109. [2]	YD 7509	S	8825	1933	W.J.King, Bishops Lydeard	1944	1965	DG6/4 T	Carried works No. 8009
110. [1]	WW 9682	A	530	1929	New	1929	1932	4	
110. [2]	WT 8294	A	476	1925	Pearson & Moody	1925	1941	4	Converted to pneumatics 1937
110. [3]	TE 9861	S	8099	1929	Sandywood Sand & Gravel Co.	1943	1964	DG6/4 T	Pneus: carried works No.8768: rebuilt as RB6
111. [1]	YL 5656	A	495	1925	Cement Marketing Co.	1930	1938	4	
111. [2]	ET 5752	S		1939		1939		4	Pneumatics: carried works plate 7933
112. [1]	KB 7896	A	43		Edmondson & Wyatt, Manchester		1933	4	
112. [2]	PW 6000	A	496	1925	W.Spruce & Son,Trowse, Norfolk	1933	1944	4	Pneumatics: last Atkinson sprayer in service
112.[3]	HD 4248	S	8335	1930	Yorkshire Dye Co. Dewsbury	1936		DG6	Pneumatics
113	TC 3059	A	387	1923	New	1923	1937	4	
114. [1]	RF 1585	A	506	1927	New	1927		4	
114. [2]	UL 5648	S	7730	1929	S. Hetton Colliery Co.		1956	DG6 T	Pneumatics
115. [1]	CK 3257	A	204	1920	Cement Marketing Co.	1930	1936	4	
115. [2]	WX 491	S	7961	1929	J. Smith, Tadcaster Brewery	1936	1954	DG4	Pneumatics
116. [1]	PW 6221	A	497	1925	Dewing & Kearsley, Fakenham	1932	1938	4	
116. [2]	WX 9803	S	8659	1932	Goole Tillage Co.	1945		DG4 T	Pneumatics
117. [1]	TU 729	A	480	1925	E.B.Ward, Stockton Heath	1932	1941	4	Rebuilt as first road burner
117. [2]	CB 9387	S	7948	1929	Kinder Bros. Blackburn	1940		DG6/4	Pneus: used as artic.unit: became RB1
118	UT 6122	S	8061	1929	W. & A. Annable, Shepsted, Leics	1936		DG4	
119. [1]	YE 8499	A	521	1927	Cement Marketing Co.	1932	1938	4	
119. [2]	YG 746	S	8694	1932	T.Sugden & Sons, Brighouse	1943	1956	DG4	Pneumatics
120	BA 5665	S	6400	1926	Topham Bros. Salford	1937	1956	Super 4	Pneumatics: used as artic.unit: RB3
121	NU 7603	A	294	1925	New	1932		4	Originally a supply tanker
122. [1]	XD 9576	Y	1401	1921	Shell Mex Ltd.	1927	1930	4	
122. [2]	NW 5043	A	406	1924	Milton & Jones	1931	1938	4	
122. [3]	NW 4206	S	7252	1927	T.Sugden & Sons, Brighouse	1944	1948	Super 4	Pneumatics
123. [1]	XD 8245	Y	1386	1921	Shell Mex Ltd.	1928	1931	4	

TABLE 1 - STEAM SPRAYERS & TANKERS

Fleet No.	Regn.No.	Make	WorksNo	Year	Previous operator	Bought	Finished	Type	Remarks
123. [2]	CK 3016	A	23	1917	John Crossley & Sons, Halifax	1931	1936	4	
123. [3]	RB 6262	S	8699	1932	Fox & Nichols, Penrith	1943	1960	DG6	Pneumatics
125	AW 7309	S	AS3190	1920	National Fuel Oil Co.			Std 4	
126. [1]	GB 7038	A						4	
126. [2]	BB 7774	S	5066	1923	J.H.Lawrenson, Whiston	1939	1956	Super 4	Pneumatics: converted to 6 wheels
127. [1]	CK 3341	A	458		Atkinson	1934	1944	4	Converted to pneus: original works No.256
127. [2]	YG 2693	S	8768	1933	Goole Tillage Co.	1946	1957	DG6/4	Pneumatics: converted to artic.RB5
128. [1]	AW 4477	S	BS 2230	1918	J.Smith, Tadcaster Brewery	1933	1938	4	
128. [2]	HB 4207	S	8730	1932	D.Thomas, Skelty, Glamorgan	1944		DG4	Pneumatics: rebuilt with extra trailing axle
129	KL 3820	A	510	1924	Cement Marketing Co.	1931		4	
137	KP 1288	S	7506	1928	Forstal Ballast, Aylesford, Kent			DG6/4 T	Pneumatics
142	TF 6711	S	8635	1931	E.B.Ward, Stockton Heath		1960	DG4	Pneumatics
143	MY 898	S	7980	1929	R.T.Warren, Southall		1965	DG4 T	Pneumatics
144	MT 3600	S	7888	1929	Ham River Grit Co		1965	DG6/4 T	Pneumatics
145	MT 3806	S	7890	1929	Ham River Grit Co.		1965	DG6/4 T	Pneumatics
146	MT 2805	S	7769	1929	Ham River Grit Co.		1965	DG6/4 T	Pneumatics
148	XP 4329	S	5141	1923	J.Lyons & Co. London		1950	Super 4	Pneumatics
154	DM 6559	S	7914	1929	Castle Fire Brick Co. Flint			DG4 T	
156	GK 5516	S	8343	1930	Cement Marketing Co.	1938	1958	DG4	Pneumatics
157	GK 131	S	8311	1930	Cement Marketing Co.	1938	1958	DG4	Pneumatics
160	YU 6560	S	7230	1927	I.G. & B.T. Phillips, Carmarthen	1941	1952	Super 4	Pneumatics
161	TE 127	C	T1150	1927	N.of E. Sand & Gravel Co.		1938		
162. [1]	TE 129	C	T1148	1927			1934	4	
162. [2]	TU 5498	F	12566	1927			1945	4	
162. [3]	HV 699	S	8284	1930	Illingworth Wood & Co.		1956	DG6	Pneumatics
164	RX 3147	S	7561	1928	F.A.Tye, East Ham	1942	1952	DG6/4 T	Pneumatics
165. [1]	WW 3736	F	12830	1927	R.M.Woolley, Bucknall	1936	1940	4	
165. [2]	GH 1422	S	8303	1930	Service Garage, Brighouse	1946	1956	DG6/4	Pneumatics
166. [1]	HW 9583	S			Annis & Co. Hayes	1948		4	Pneumatics
166. [2]	OD 1572	S	8666	1932	W.Elworthy, Tiverton			DG4	Pneumatics
167	GJ 1446	S	8273	1930	Cement Marketing Co.	1938	1957	DG6/4	Pneumatics
168	TY 9994	S	8396	1930	Lewis, Knox & Prior, Birtley	1952		4	Pneumatics
169	GW 2938	S	8681	1932	A.H.&E.Foster, London	1948	1965	DG4	Pneumatics
170	TE 9662	S	8070	1929	Heaton Mills Bleaching Co.		1963	DG6/4 T	Pneumatics
171. [1]	UT 5845	S	8009	1929	Concrete Ltd. London SW6	1942		DG4	Pneumatics: rebuilt as artic.unit
171. [2]	XH 5836	S	8385	1930	Latham & Co. London		1955	DG4	Pneumatics
172. [1]	GN 5753	S	8452	1931	Annis & Co. Hayes	1952	1965	DG6/4	Pneus: carried works No.8696: rebuilt as RB2
172. [2]	VO 7828	S	8696	1932	T.Curtis, Hounslow	1951	1965	DG6/4	Pneumatics: rebuilt as artic. unit
173	TF 3618	S	8377	1930	J.Morris, Liverpool	1950	1956	DG4 T	Pneumatics: rebuilt as artic. unit
174	LG 7418	S	8543	1931	Sir R. McAlpine, EllesmerePort	1939	1956	DG6/4	Pneumatics

TABLE 1 - STEAM SPRAYERS & TANKERS

The fleet numbers of the following eighteen sprayers have not been identified.

Fleet No.	Regn.No.	Make	WorksNo	Year	Previous operator	Bought	Finished	Type	Remarks
	WT 9590	A	373		Atkinsons	1928	1931	4	
	EC 5314	A	434	1924	N.Bennett, Ambleside		1931	4	Burnt out, 1931
	KU 4239	A		1924	Greenhill Mills			4	
	BA 4289	A		1924	A.M.K.Flint, Salford	1933		4	
	UT 1555	A	519	1927	Glenfield Haulage Co.Ltd.	1934	1942	4	
	TD 6996	L	F2/120	1926			1932	4	
	AW 3095	S		1916			1938	4	
	AW 7427	S	AS 3211	1920	National Fuel Oil Co.			4	
	AW 8247	S	AS 3482	1920	National Fuel Oil Co.		1941	4	
	WA 7665	S			P.Andrew, Pendleton	1934		4	
	HL 1791	S	5188	1924	F.Mitchell, Ossett	1939	1940	4	
	CP 4644	S	6447	1926	Hartley & Sugden, Halifax		1938	Super 4	
	BA 6254	S	6814	1926	Topham Bros. Salford	1939		Super 4	Pneumatics
	VY 36	S	7517	1928	J.J.Hunt, York	1937	1940	Super 4	
	DG 1987	S	8491	1931	E.Spencer, Liverpool	1942		DG4	Pneumatics
	GT 2827	S	8590	1931	Bit. Road Products, Middlesbrough	1946	1962	DG6	Pneumatics
	RH 4589	S	8647	1932	Bit. Road Products, Middlesbrough	1946	1962	DG4	Pneumatics
	PV 31	S	8726	1932	Mitchell &Butlers, Birmingham	1946	1962	DG4	Pneumatics

Notes
DG6/4 denotes that the wagon was originally six-wheeled but was converted to four-wheeled.
The addition of T means it was a tipper when bought.
Dates in italics are probable but unproven.
Wagons on pneumatics are so described in the Remarks column (pneumatics is shortened to pneus where space is pressing).
Other wagons were on solid rubbers.

TABLE 2 - OTHER STEAM WAGONS

Regn.No.	Make	WorksNo	Year	Previous operator	Bought	Finished	Type	Remarks
CK 3120	A	132	1919	Cement Marketing Co.	1931	1931	4	Possibly used to rebuild Atkinson EC5314
CB 4176	A	389	1923	Service Garage, Brighouse	1938	1938	4	
FE 3608	CS	48022	1917	New from makers	1917	1936	4	
FE 3609	CS	47987	1917	New from makers	1917	1936	4	
FE 1827	CS	47349	1915	York Corporation		1936	4	
TE 141	C	T1149	1927			1937	4	Possibly a sprayer
M 2079	F	1720	1908	J.Graven, Ely	1917	1925	4	
AR 7501	F	4084	1913	War Dept.	1921	1930	4	
M 9234	F	7066	1917	P.Andrew, Pendleton	1938	1938	4	
EN 2369	F	11170	1925	P.Andrew, Pendleton	1938	1938	4	
EN 2701	F	12090	1925	P.Andrew, Pendleton	1938	1938	4	
TE 2186	F	12798	1927	S.T.Rosbotham, Bickerstaffe	1938	1939	4	
AW 8632	S	3628	1920	P.Andrew, Pendleton	1938	1938	4	Pneumatics
DH 3282	S		1923	P.Andrew, Pendleton	1938	1938	4	Pneumatics; [No. between 4356 and4359]
TX 1941	S	6708	1926	A.John, Rhydyfelin	1941		Super 4	
TX 2848	S	6922	1927	A.John, Rhydyfelin	1941		Super 4	
KO 8877	S	7321	1928	Forstal Ballast, Aylesford	1938		DG6 T	
CB 8176	S	7423	1928	Kinder Bros. Blackburn	1938	1938	DG6	
UX 2860	S	7438	1928	Johnston Bros. Dawley	1937		DG6 T	Pneumatics: believed converted to sprayer
DM 6593	S	7917	1929	Castle Fire Brick, Northop, Flint			DG6	
UX 4944	S	7933	1929	H.Hirst, Nelson			DG6	Used to rebuild no.111 and works No. transferred
GC 7436	S	8200	1930	Annis & Co., Hayes	1946	1956	DG6	Believed to have been converted to sprayer
GE 9218	S	8259	1930	L.&W.Cole, Leeds	1944		DG4	
KX 5200	S	8289	1930	W.J.King, Bishops Lydeard	1938		DG4 T	
GH 5447	S	8344	1930	Cement Marketing Co.	1938	1939	DG4	
GP 8880	S	8560	1931	Annis & Co., Hayes	1947		DG6	Pneumatics: not licensed by Glossops
GT 1566	S	8570	1931	Annis & Co., Hayes	1946	1953	DG6	Pneumatics
GT 2013	S	8583	1931	Annis & Co., Hayes	1946	1953	DG6	Pneumatics
LG 7423	S	8600	1931	Sir R.McAlpine, Ellesmere Port	1939		DG4	Pneumatics
LG 7905	S	8625	1931	Spillers Ltd.	1946		DG4	Pneumatics
GX 902	S	8652	1932	Annis & Co., Hayes	1946	late 50s	DG6	Pneumatics
DM 7845	S	8705	1932	F.M.Clements, Wrexham	1946		DG4	Pneumatics
TF 9228	S	8728	1932	Brookes & Co., Manchester		1952	DG6	Pneumatics
YD 7510	S	8824	1933	W.J.King, Bishops Lydeard	1945	1952	DG6	Pneumatics
AUC 914	S	8872	1933	Annis & Co., Hayes	1946		S4	Based at Mitcham depot: doubtful if used.
AUC 915	S	8873	1934	Annis & Co., Hayes	1946		S4	Based at Mitcham depot: doubtful if used.
AUC 916	S	8874	1934	Annis & Co., Hayes	1946		S4	Based at Mitcham depot: doubtful if used.
AUC 908	S	8878	1933	Annis & Co., Hayes	1946		S6	Based at Mitcham depot: doubtful if used.

TABLE 2 - OTHER STEAM WAGONS

Regn.No.	Make	WorksNo	Year	Previous operator	Bought	Finished	Type	Remarks
AUC 909	S	8879	1933	Annis & Co., Hayes	1946		S6	Based at Mitcham depot: doubtful if used.
AUC 910	S	8880	1933	Annis & Co., Hayes	1946		S6	Based at Mitcham depot: doubtful if used.
AUC 911	S	8881	1933	Annis & Co., Hayes	1946		S6	Based at Mitcham depot: doubtful if used.
U 5179	Y	1169	1919	G.Shellabear, Plymouth	1931		4	Not used on the road

TABLE 3- STEAM ROLLERS & TRACTION ENGINES

Regn.No.	Make	WorksNo.	Type	Year	Previous operator	Bought	Ended	Remarks
PY 8274	A&P		12½T CDO	1899		by1943	1951	
TD 1957	A&P	4341	10T CDO	1901	Halifax Corporation	by1943		
CP 2245	A&P	4744	10T S	1902	Rowley Plant	by1943	1948	
FX 6938	A&P	4988	10T CDS	1905	Otley UDC		1964	
WR 7329	A&P	5805	6½T CDS	1906	E.Parry & Co., London	1945	1949	
D 1264	A&P	6031	10T CDP	1919	G.Roberts, Caistor	1933		
CA 7850	A&P	9080	10T CDP	1923	York Corporation	1933	1952	
DN 2003	A&P	10674	10T CDP	1925	Barnes Corporation	1938	1951	
PE 7095	A&P	11212	12T CDS	1905	W.Thackray, Old Malton, Yorks	1938	1946	Sold to Thames Tar Products, Mitcham
WR 7188	TG	1485	10½T S	1911	Otty Bros., Horsforth	1935	1941	
WR 6555	TG	1659	10T CDS	1915	C.H.Johnson, Ripon		1940	
WR 6551	TG	1870	15T CDO	1903	Leeds Corporation	1931	1949	Sold to J.W.Stafford
U 8427	JF	9703	8T CDS	1919	Flaxton RDC, Yorks	1938	1943	
AJ 3952	ML	72097	8T CDS	1921	Cardiff Corporation		1942	
BO 3852	ML	74191	8T SP	1927	Beddington & Wallington UDC			
PH 1139	ML	82101	6hpTE single	1934	W.Thackray, Old Malton, Yorks	1937	1946	Sold to Thames Tar Products, Mitcham
TL 3612	ML	87003	8T CDS		J.Allen & Sons, Oxford	1953	1955	Sold to J.R.Hardy
BW 4838	W&S		8T CDS	1909			1942	
AA 2294	W&S	7081	8T CDS	1917	War Dept.	1939	1944	
BT 3558	W&S	7456	6hpTE single	1926	E.Parry & Co., London	1922		
HO 6472	W&S	7832	Simplicity	1927	York Corporation	1933	1959	
DN 2005	W&S	7941	Advance				1969	For tarmac plant at Chelsea Basin. Expn.gear

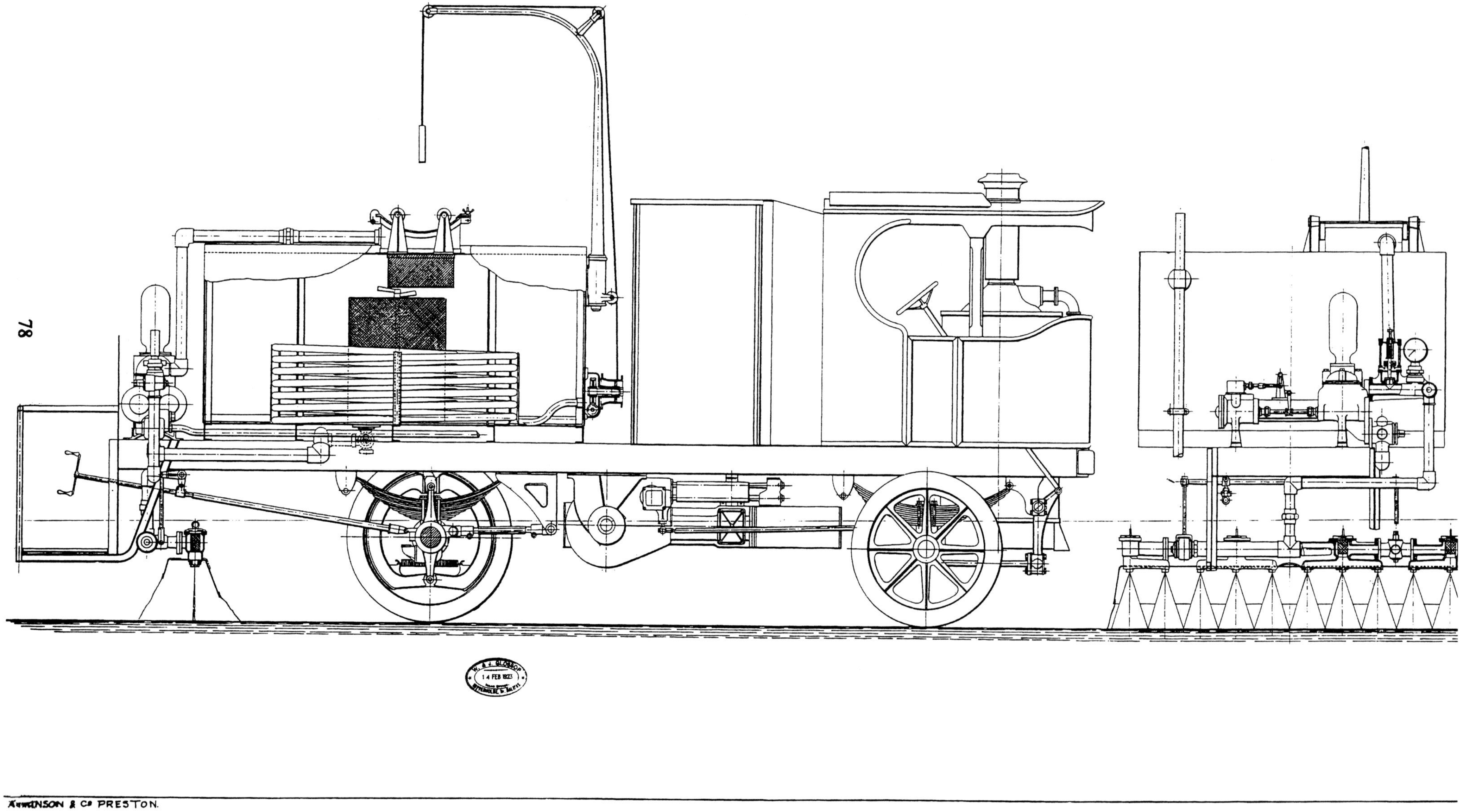

ATKINSON & C⁰ PRESTON.

Fig. 67. The Atkinson drawing showing sprayer No.102. No.101 differed in having the makers standard water tank which was lower than that shown.

THE "ATKINSON-UNIFLOW" BITUMEN SPRAYER.

(PATENT APPLIED FOR)

Fig.68. *Sprayers Nos.104 and 105 were originally designed, as in this drawing, to carry Atkinson's design of bitumen sprayer on which the tank was heated by a coal fire rather than by steam coils. The bitumen was applied by combination nozzles in which the compressed air from the steam driven pump nebulised the hot bitumen delivered separately to the nozzles.*

Fig.69. *The Wallis & Steevens Advance roller (works No.7941 of 1927) bought from York Corporation and operated from Osbaldwick depot until 1969, making it the last Glossop steam vehicle in use. In this photograph by the late Alfred Bennett it is in an A64 lay-by not far from York.* [John Knapton / Eric Robinson collection]

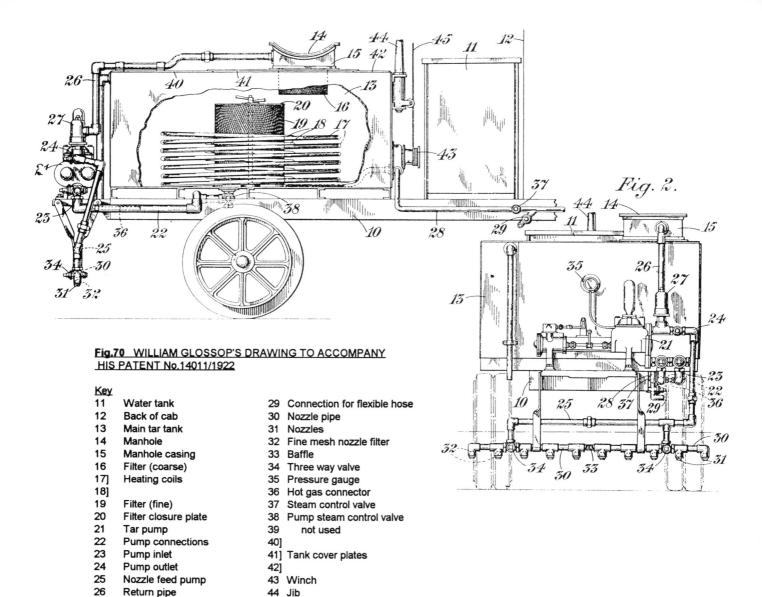

Fig.70 WILLIAM GLOSSOP'S DRAWING TO ACCOMPANY
 HIS PATENT No.14011/1922

Key

11	Water tank	29	Connection for flexible hose
12	Back of cab	30	Nozzle pipe
13	Main tar tank	31	Nozzles
14	Manhole	32	Fine mesh nozzle filter
15	Manhole casing	33	Baffle
16	Filter (coarse)	34	Three way valve
17]	Heating coils	35	Pressure gauge
18]		36	Hot gas connector
19	Filter (fine)	37	Steam control valve
20	Filter closure plate	38	Pump steam control valve
21	Tar pump	39	not used
22	Pump connections	40]	
23	Pump inlet	41]	Tank cover plates
24	Pump outlet	42]	
25	Nozzle feed pump	43	Winch
26	Return pipe	44	Jib
27	Relief valve	45	Barrel hoisting cable
28	Steam pipe connections		

Other books by R.A.Whitehead

¶ denotes still in print

The Story of the Colne Valley (jointly with F.D.Simpson)	Oakwood Press [Reprint]
Garretts of Leiston	Percival Marshall
A Century of Service	Eddison Plant
The Age of the Traction Engine	Ian Allan
A Century of Steam Rolling	Ian Allan
Steam in the Village	David & Charles
Garrett 200	Transport Bookman
Kaleidoscope of Steam Wagons	Marshall Harris & Baldwin
Kaleidoscope of Traction Engines	Marshall Harris & Baldwin
Wallis & Steevens - a History	R.L.S.
¶ *A Review of Steam Tractors*	R.L.S.
¶ *Austrian Steam Locomotives 1837-1981*	R.A.Whitehead & Partners
The Beloved Coast & the Suffolk Sandlings	Terence Dalton
Jesse Ellis & the Maidstone Wagons	R.A.Whitehead & Partners
Steam is the Essence	R.A.Whitehead & Partners
¶ *Garrett Diesel Tractors*	R.A.Whitehead & Partners
¶ *Made by Garretts*	R.A.Whitehead & Partners
¶ *Garrett Wagons Part 1 - Pioneers & Overtypes*	R.A.Whitehead & Partners
¶ *Garrett Wagons Part 2 - Undertypes*	R.A.Whitehead & Partners
¶ *Garrett Wagons Part 3 - Electrics & Motors*	R.A.Whitehead & Partners
¶ *Garrett Traction & Ploughing Engines*	R.A.Whitehead & Partners
¶ *Garrett Steam Tractors & Rollers*	R.A.Whitehead & Partners